Praise for *A Polyamory Devotional*

"'Vita doesn't pull any punches with her raw and deeply
personal perspective. A year of her daily takes is definitely a
learning experience that all of us can get something from."
—Kevin A. Patterson, M.Ed., author of *Love's Not Color Blind: Race and
Representation in Polyamorous and Other Alternative Communities*

"*In* A Polyamory Devotional, *Evita 'Lavitaloca' Sawyers offers
a wealth of rich, bite-sized daily reflections to support you
on your consensual nonmonogamy journey. Her practical
wisdom and experience-based insights are a must-read!*"
—Jessica Fern, author of *Polysecure: Attachment, Trauma and Consensual
Nonmonogamy* and *Polywise: A Deeper Dive into Navigating Open Relationships*

"As refreshingly authentic and thoughtful as the woman who wrote it.
Reading through each day's prompts felt like listening to a good friend
tell you that they've been through the same struggles you are facing,
while gently nudging you in the direction of self-reflection, introspection
and personal betterment. I found myself bookmarking specific prompts
that reminded me of the things that needed work in my own relationships
so I could return to them whenever I wanted a comforting reminder."
—Emily Sotelo Matlack, co-host of the Multiamory podcast and
co-author of *Multiamory: Essential Tools for Modern Relationships*

"Evita answers the question my nonmonogamous clients most often
ask at the start of therapy: where should we begin? Begin here,
with this devotional. Evita offers insightful, digestible, actionable
prompts for engaging with polyamory, one day at a time."
—Casey Tanner, queer sex therapist and creator of The Expansive Group

"Through her challenges and missteps, Evita compassionately teaches us how to deal with hard feelings, navigate sovereignty and open our hearts to love more than one person. These daily reflections provide not only the tools but the hope that we can all gain growth, unlearn harmful relationship beliefs and develop deeper self-awareness through the consensual nonmonogamy journey. The wisdom in this book deserves a Ph.D."
—Evalene (Evelin) Molina Dacker, MD, family physician and creator of the STARS Talk framework for sexual communication

"Whether you're just beginning your polyamory journey or you've been living a polyamorous life for decades, these daily reads will help you approach your relationships in a mindful and constructive way. Evita has this amazing ability to take complex, overwhelming concepts and bring them down to earth. Her reflections are nice and bite-sized while still being very rich. Polyamory is a constant process, and this book is the perfect format to help anyone along the journey."
—Chad "polyamfam" Spangler, polyamorous entertainer and educator

"Reading through each page feels like a baptism to the parts of my soul that fear the dismantling of everything that nonmonogamy forces you to confront within yourself. This book is a true blessing, allowing the reader to have the guidance of Evita as a shepherd as they climb the proverbial mountain of polyamory."
—Jessica Daylover, writer of the Remodeled Love blog and co-author of *Polyamory and Parenthood.*

"Empathetic, witty and engaging, A Polyamory Devotional *is accessible to people new to polyamory, as well as those who are long-time nonmonogamists. Rather than telling people how they should be, it provides insights into Sawyers's personal journey, tidbits of wisdom and questions to spur readers' personal contemplations."*
—Dr. Elisabeth "Eli" Sheff, author of *The Polyamorists Next Door* and *Children in Polyamorous Families*

A
POLYAMORY
DEVOTIONAL

A
POLYAMORY
DEVOTIONAL

365 Daily Reflections for the Consensually Nonmonogamous

Evita *Lavitaloca* Sawyers

with a foreword by
Chaneé Jackson Kendall

THORNAPPLE
PRESS

Thornapple Press ✒ 300 – 722 Cormorant Street ✳ Victoria, BC
V8W 1P8 Canada ✳ press@thornapplepress.ca

Thornapple Press is a brand of Talk Science to Me Communications Inc. and the
successor to Thorntree Press. Our business offices are located in the traditional,
ancestral and unceded territories of the ləkʷəŋən and W̱SÁNEĆ peoples.

Cover and interior design by Jeff Werner ✳ Substantive editing by Andrea Zanin
Copy-editing by Hazel Boydell ✒ Proofreading by Heather van der Hoop
Illustrations by Tikva Wolf

Library and Archives Canada Cataloguing in Publication
Title: A polyamory devotional :
365 daily reflections for the consensually nonmonogamous /
Evita Lavitaloca Sawyers ; with a foreword by Chaneé Jackson Kendall.
Names: Sawyers, Evita Lavitaloca, author.
Description: Includes index.
Identifiers: Canadiana (print) 20230183956 |
Canadiana (ebook) 20230184014 |
ISBN 9781990869235 (softcover) |
ISBN 9781990869242 (EPUB)
Subjects: LCSH: Non-monogamous relationships.
Classification: LCC HQ980 .S29 2023 | DDC 306.84/23–dc23

10   9   8   7   6   5   4   3   2   1

Printed in the United States of America.

To my children: Polyamory helped me learn how to love you more freely and for that I am forever grateful. May my love always feel like a magic carpet ride to you.

To all my partners, past, present and future:
Your presence is in these pages and in my heart.
Thank you for the love and the lessons.

Foreword

"What up fam? It's ya girl, 'Vita. Hey, how you doin?"

With this iconic greeting, we are introduced to one of modern-day polyamory's most prolific voices. Although she has become well-known for her popular Instagram posts under the title "Today's Polyamory Reminder," my initial introduction to Evita Sawyers's raspy yet upbeat contralto and larger-than-life personality came in 2016 via the documentary *Poly Love* and her subsequent YouTube videos, in which she openly discussed our lovestyle and its joys and challenges. Although it is now my privilege to write this foreword from my perspective as a polyamorous educator, activist and event planner, when I first saw *Poly Love*, I was a Black, queer, polyamorous new mom in a nested triad. In 'Vita's experience, I saw myself—at the intersection of all these marginalized identities—for the first time ever.

My journey did not begin as an intentional one—I simply fell in love with multiple people and had no desire to lie about it, cover it up or love and be loved in the shadows. I had no idea that this single act of defiance would take me on an exhilarating voyage of self-discovery and love that continues to change my life in immeasurable ways. I now understand that encountering Evita was a pivotal moment that would inform, enrich and fundamentally alter the personal and professional trajectory of my life.

At this point, I had just begun to seek polyamorous community. I'd joined Facebook groups and was looking for "my people." In one of these small but burgeoning Black polyamorous groups, I e-met Evita. At that time, she was still reeling from the breakup of the triad featured in the documentary, which led to our initial exchanges being peppered with disagreements and differences in ideology. These early conversations laid the groundwork for a personal and professional connection that has not only upgraded the quality of my life, but has also served as the catalyst for several educational initiatives in the polyamorous community. The most notable of these initiatives is The Metamour Bill of Rights.

In the early days of our polyamorous education and community building, interactions that began as kikis in Facebook comment sections morphed into inbox conversations that flowed effortlessly into early-morning phone calls and video chats. In these calls, we discussed our lives, our loves and the way polyamory was changing us. We created a space of friendship, radical vulnerability and care that we still enjoy. I am delighted that this book is now available to create a similar space for polyamorists all over the world.

Evita's unwavering commitment to being exactly who she is—for better or for worse—has always been her most outstanding quality. When I consult my friend and colleague about my relationships, I am assured that I will receive an honest, balanced assessment of the situation that is focused on what I need to hear, not just what I want to hear. Her analysis is always caring, often humorous and uncannily well-timed. You will encounter this same tone in the pages of this book.

In a lot of ways, Evita is the embodiment of "normalizing" polyamory. She is neither perfect nor immune from normal human emotions, and she makes zero effort to be. Her unwavering realness is truly where her magic lies. She owns up to her weaknesses, thoughtfully interrogates her mistakes and offers grace to herself and others—all in her witty, matter-of-fact style, which is both deeply introspective and to the point.

Through this book, you get to benefit from the thoughtfulness, wisdom and experience of Evita Sawyers, and you will be forever changed. She has a way of cutting to the heart of every matter, expertly deciphering the innermost fears that bring us either closer or farther away from radical self-love and, by extension, love for others. Her self-reflection is evident in each day's prompt. Even when we're experiencing relationship conflict, she simultaneously comforts our hearts and challenges us to be self-reflective.

As you read this book, and when you later revisit the daily prompts during times of stress or struggle in your relationships, I hope that you hear my friend's signature voice in your head encouraging you to love yourself and others and reminding you to show up to your life and relationships as your best self.

— Chaneé Jackson Kendall,
polyamorous educator, speaker,
activist and event planner

Acknowledgments

I am sheepish to admit that I Googled "How to write an acknowledgment for a book" because I was afraid that I wouldn't do it right. How do I distill the gratitude I have for the countless humans who made this book possible into a few short lines? I'm going to try to do my best though, and if I miss some folks, judge my head and not my heart.

I would first like to thank my children. I sometimes think that the universe brought me to polyamory so I could learn how to love them better. It is a joy to be your mother and to continue to learn how to freely love and honor your personhood.

I would like to acknowledge every partner, lover, crush and romantic interest I have ever had. I wouldn't have been able to learn these lessons were it not for my experiences with them. I want to thank them for being my teachers, my former spouse especially. I am in gratitude to you.

I want to thank my friends—for cheering me on, for our amazingly profound conversations that inspired some of these reflections, for being my people. Special shout out to Chelsea, Ardis, Manijeh, Elle, Monica, CJ, Malika, Julian, Tre, Cindy and Maharani. Also, to Courtney and Jhos because they opened their home in Ecuador to me, which is where a lot of the book was written. Thank you for being soul family.

Thank you also to Tikva Wolf for the illustrations and for making my entire world more colorful simply by being who they are. Thank you to all my metamours, both the ones I liked and the ones I didn't care for, because you also taught me valuable lessons that are reflected here. Special mention to Roselyn and Nikki because they are gifts.

To Eve Rickert and the Thornapple Press crew: Thank you for taking a chance on me. I can't begin to express how surreal publishing a book is for me.

To my followers: I LOVE Y'ALL! Thank you for your support.

To Ron Young, Ruby Bouie Johnson, Michelle Flores and anyone who has given me a platform to speak, share and educate: Thank you for believing in the power of my voice.

To my ancestors and deities and spirit guides: Thank you for covering me and granting me your divine wisdoms. Special acknowledgment to Thoth for blessing my writing.

To my momma because she's the best.

And lastly, in the fashion of Issa Rae during her 2019 Women in Film Awards acceptance speech, I'd like to acknowledge my damn self. 'Vita, you did that. You wrote a whole damn book with your magical ass. Never doubt what you are capable of.

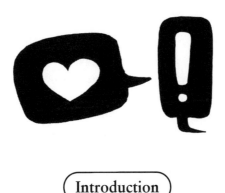

Introduction

What up, fam? It's ya girl, 'Vita.

I'm a forty-year-old Black, queer mother of three who is currently going through a divorce and who has been practicing nonmonogamy for the last decade. To say I am humbled and grateful that you and I are here together, connecting via this book, is an understatement. Truth is, I don't enjoy writing and certainly never thought I would write enough to create a book. What started as personal social media posts and a pandemic experiment has turned into the body of work that you are currently holding.

My entry into polyamory and ethical nonmonogamy was *rough*. I struggled. A lot. I didn't understand why everyone seemed to be "better" at this than I was. And so, I began talking. First, my words were just cries for help. I would post in online polyamory groups asking for advice on how to navigate all the challenging emotions I was experiencing while trying to shift from a lifetime of monogamy to ethical nonmonogamy. I wanted to know if there was anyone out there who could help me figure out how to do this. Then, my words became confessions. I started to share my experiences. I would post my reflections and my process through my difficult emotions in practicing nonmonogamy on my personal Facebook page and in various online polyamory groups. I talked about my discomforts, my jealousies, my mistakes and my experiences of fumbling through learning how to live and love this way. I shared my struggles in learning how to release my control and my desire to limit my partners, and the lessons I learned about myself along the way. My thought was, "If I can help just *one* person not have to go through what I'm going through, help them feel less alone, it's worth it." I developed a reputation for being a person who was willing to share the things that people were afraid to admit to themselves, let alone others. Gradually, folks started to send me messages about how much they appreciated my willingness to talk about my experiences because they mirrored their own and helped them to feel less alienated.

That led to requests to appear on podcasts, to speak at conferences and even led to a 2016 documentary film, *Poly Love*, about my relationship with my then husband and a partner we had at the time. People appreciated my openness about the good, the bad and the ugly parts of living an ethically nonmonogamous life. And since so much of the public face and voice of polyamory was from a white perspective, the fact that I was a Black polyamorous woman being so unapologetically open and vocal about it was revolutionary. People appreciated my frank and balanced wisdom, my candor and my willingness to acknowledge my mistakes. Both friends and people I didn't know personally would reach out to me to get my advice on the various situations they were struggling with.

When the COVID-19 pandemic hit, I had been laid off from my job and was stuck in the house. I challenged myself to see if I could come up with a daily piece of polyamory wisdom to share with my followers. I also began offering peer support, guidance and coaching to folks who desired my advice, since

I was already doing that informally anyway. That experiment struck a chord as more and more people were discovering nonmonogamy and seeking resources and guidance on how to live this way. I went from having a relatively small following to now having over 40,000 followers on various platforms, all interacting with and reflecting on the content I create.

I've heard a range of feedback about the value of my voice—appreciation of the fact that I'm a Black, queer woman who is open and unapologetic about being polyamorous, of me being a mother who is polyamorous and for my commitment to asserting that it's OK to be human in polyamory. But what makes this whole project most worthwhile is when someone reaches out to tell me that reading one of my posts enabled them to take their first deep breath in days, that my post gave them the courage they needed to stand up for themselves or that I gave voice to their heart. Being able to be for others what I needed for myself when I was struggling has been an indescribable blessing.

This book was born from that desire—I intend it to be what you need at the time when you need it. You can read it daily or you can pick it up when you remember to. You can mark certain pages that speak to you and come back to them later. The idea is that reading the daily passages will inspire you to reflect on yourself and to initiate conversations with your partners about the ideas. I hope you find yourself and your loved ones in the pages. Not everything will resonate with you and your experience, and that's OK. Pay attention to what comes forward in your body and in your heart as you read. Look into the parts of yourself that may experience discomfort. Listen to your inner voice as you are hearing from mine. What you have to say to *yourself* is just as important as anything written here.

The advice in this book is "good faith" advice, meaning that it comes with the assumption that you are in mostly healthy, loving relationships with people who aren't being intentionally harmful or abusive and are reasonable human beings. If you are in a situation where you are being abused or treated poorly, all the advice in the world won't be able to fix that. If you are in a situation where you are being abused or being treated poorly, I want to emphasize that you do not deserve that. I hope you find the strength to leave that situation and seek healing. Talk to a professional, lean on the people in your life who love you and want the best for you and gather the strength and courage you need to walk away. I know that we can sometimes conflate love with pain, especially if our life experiences or our families of origin have made them synonymous, but true love is a healing safe space for you to rest and bloom in, not one where you will be struck down and harmed.

These daily wisdoms came from the school of hard knocks. These pages are filled with my stories, my joys, my pains, my triumphs and my mistakes. I am immensely grateful for your willingness to witness them. Thank you.

Polyamory is an individual journey.

I used to love a song by Sara Groves called "This Journey Is My Own," and indeed, this has been my experience of nonmonogamy. Though I started along this journey with a partner, I had a very different experience from them. I had my own unique struggles and challenges and learned what mattered most to *me* about relationships. ❧ Even if you enter nonmonogamy as a couple, you will have a different experience from your partner and will likely discover that you each want different things from it. Even if you date the same person together, you will each have a unique experience with that person. If you enter nonmonogamy as a single person, you will have to get deeply in touch with yourself to be clear on what you genuinely want from relationships. Your path may run parallel to the paths of your partners, but it will be separate. This is a journey of immense self-discovery. ❧ For couples entering polyamory, this may be the first time that they "separate" and see themselves as two individuals with different desires, perspectives and relationship values who happen to be in a relationship with one another, rather than as joined together or as "one flesh." This can be scary but also liberating. ❧ The most important relationship we will ever have in life is the one we have with ourselves.

How has polyamory been an individual journey for you? What have you personally discovered about yourself as it relates to nonmonogamy?

Day 2

Relationship structures are meant to serve the people in them. When the needs of the people change, the likelihood of success is greater when they seek to change the structure, not the people.

Think of a relationship like a house and the people in that relationship as the inhabitants of the house. When these people initially moved into the house, it fit whatever needs they had at the time. As life progressed, their needs may have changed. Maybe the house was no longer big enough for them, or perhaps it began to feel too big. Maybe the people in the house realized they couldn't live together all the time, or even at all. When such a scenario happens, you are likely to have a happier outcome by finding a new home that suits the needs of everyone living in it than by trying to change the perspectives of the people who live in the house. ❧ Our relationships are like houses that we occupy with our partners. When our needs or our partners' needs change, we have a much better chance of success if we reimagine the relationship structure instead of trying to change ourselves or our partners to fit a structure that isn't working for us. Collaborating to find a new structure that works for everyone is far more effective than trying to make yourself or your partners live in a house that no longer serves your needs.

How do the relationship structures you're in serve your current relationship needs?

It's important that we are collaborating with each of our partners to establish what being committed to one another means to us, and that we understand that what signifies commitment in one relationship may not be the same as what signifies commitment in another.

Exclusivity, marriage, shared home and finances, children—these are some of the things that society holds as markers of committed relationships. When we enter the world of polyamory, we can find ourselves in relationships where all or some or none of these things are a part of our partnerships. As such, it can be hard to arrive at a feeling of security with someone when you struggle to identify things that signify you are committed to one another. ❀ It is important to be in conversation and collaboration with each of your partners on what the unique commitment you have to each other is. It is equally important to understand that commitment won't necessarily look the same for each relationship. You may have a partner for whom commitment looks like the traditional ideas of shared property and children, and another partner for whom it looks like something totally different. It can be hard to weave in and out of your various commitment spaces and still feel an overall sense of security in your relationships. ❀ Having conversations and partnering on a shared definition of commitment with your partners is crucial for you and for them.

What does commitment mean to you?

Day 4

It is not necessary to completely understand a person's emotions in order to offer them care and empathy.

I'm not a dog person at all but my best friend loves her dogs immensely. Recently, she had to put down her beloved dog, Yuki, whom she had since she was a puppy. She was devastated. I didn't understand the love she had for her dog, but I did understand how sad she was about losing her. I was able to be empathetic and caring to her in her grief, even though it wasn't something I had experienced. ❧ Sometimes, partners express an emotion and try though you might, you can't understand why they are feeling that way. Maybe they are feeling jealous and you aren't a particularly jealous person. Maybe they are feeling threatened by your new love and you don't understand why because you love all of your partners. Maybe they are feeling triggered by a situation that reminds them of a hurtful past experience and you don't understand that because you haven't had that experience. While I believe it is important to try to understand our partners' emotions, showing care and empathy for them is far more valuable and important. ❧ You won't be able to understand every emotion your loved ones have, but that doesn't mean you can't be empathetic toward them. It's saying, "I don't understand what you're going through but I can tell that you are hurting and that matters to me."

Which do you find to be most important to you when communicating difficult emotions: being empathized with or being understood?

If you asked your partner for reassurance, a particular consideration or kind of care in nonmonogamy, don't reject it when they give it to you by declaring that they are only doing it because you asked them to or so they can be with others.

Not only is this hurtful to our partners, it's also confusing. You tell your partner, "Here is something you can do to show care for me as you are relating to others," but when they give you the thing you asked for, you swat it away by accusing them of only doing it to get to be with others or because you asked them to, not because they want to. It makes your partner feel damned if they do or damned if they don't. ❧ If your partner is showing up and giving you what you are asking for, show gratitude. Thank them for listening to you and responding with the direct support you need. If you find that what you asked for doesn't work for you, tell them that and try to find other ways they can support you. It's unfair to penalize them for giving you what you said you wanted. It makes it hard to trust what you say and leads to your partners' feeling exasperated in their relationship with you.

Do you sometimes find it difficult to accept the care that you asked your partners to give you? If so, why?

Don't agree to considerations, accommodations and acts of care that you don't genuinely desire to give out of a sense of obligation to your partners.

Sometimes our partners make requests of us that we can't or don't want to give to them. In such instances, we need to be honest with them. Say something like, "I understand you may want or need this, but I am not able or willing to provide that. Is there something else we can come up with together that gives you what you need and is also something I am willing and capable of doing?" ❧ This way, what you are giving feels truly authentic. When you are giving someone something that they know you don't really want to give or isn't in your nature to give, it feels disingenuous and gets in the way of their ability to receive it. Don't make agreements you know you don't want to keep, don't agree to considerations you don't truly want to make, and don't agree to provide things you don't wish to. All that breeds is resentment. Collaborate with your partners to find ways that you can meet their desires and needs that are in alignment with what you genuinely and naturally wish to provide.

Do you sometimes find yourself agreeing to give your partners considerations that you don't want to or can't provide? What makes it hard for you to say no?

Changing your perception of jealousy goes a long way in changing your experience of it.

Jealousy isn't an enemy emotion. It is a friend and a remarkable tool for self-discovery. ❧ I love the poem "The Guest House" by Rumi, which encourages the reader to welcome all "unexpected visitors," even if they're "a crowd of sorrows, who violently sweep your house empty of its furniture." Jealousy is not an enemy that seeks to tear apart your relationships or make you feel bad. It's a message from our innermost selves trying to alert us to a need we have, a healing that needs to take place, a calling to go deeper in our awareness of ourselves. When I stopped seeing it as an adversary and started viewing it as an ally, it changed my entire experience with it.

Is jealousy a friend or an enemy emotion to you?

Day 8

It can be true both that we did the best we could and for our best not to result in the outcome we wanted. Learning to hold these truths simultaneously can help you move on and be at peace with yourself and what happened.

Many of us try so hard to be the perfect polyamorous partner. We don't get jealous, we are comfortable with our partners' other relationships, we express our wants and needs in clear and vulnerable language, and yet sometimes, we fall short of our standards for ourselves, make mistakes, or encounter a perfect storm of circumstances that makes it difficult for us to meet our target. When that happens, the result can be an outcome we didn't want. We can damage a relationship, hurt someone we love or disappoint ourselves. We can do our best and still not produce what we wanted. ❧ Say you had a rough day, and in the evening your partner is going on a date with a new person. You want to be compersive and excited for them, but you're irritated and feeling insecure and you snap at them. As a result, your partner tells you they need a few days of space before connecting with you again. While you can (and should) own that you were wrong to snap at them, you were spent and did the best you could at that time. You weren't trying to hurt them, but nevertheless they got hurt and need space to care for themselves. Both of these things are valid. ❧ You did all you could, but sometimes that isn't enough. That's OK—that's life. However, remember that acknowledging this doesn't negate the need to examine where you could improve or learn for next time.

What makes it difficult for you to accept that you did your best when the outcome of a situation isn't what you intended?

Being a "good partner" in nonmonogamy doesn't mean figuring out how to never have difficult emotions or never struggling with our partners' choices. It means being honest, kind, compassionate, accountable, understanding, gracious and committed to moving in integrity and love even during the challenges and struggles.

There are so many opinions on what being a "good partner" in nonmonogamy is, and we often judge ourselves when we don't measure up to these ideas. When we find ourselves feeling jealous or struggling with uncomfortable emotions or needing more reassurance than we'd like to from our partners, we can make ourselves feel worse by telling ourselves we aren't being a "good" partner. But being a good partner isn't about being the "perfect polyamorous partner." It's about being honest, empathetic, kind, compassionate, loving and respectful, both to our partners and to ourselves. ❧ Having challenges as we navigate nonmonogamy doesn't make us a "bad" partner. It's how we show up to our partners and ourselves in the face of those challenges that counts.

In what ways do you judge yourself as being a "bad" partner in polyamory?

Uncomfortable feelings in nonmonogamy can feel so visceral and urgent that you may feel you have to deal with them right away, but in reality it can be best to pause and gain clarity.

This is a lesson that I learned over the course of my journey. I would experience a situation that generated difficult emotions and would be so uncomfortable that I wanted to deal with it right away just to get rid of them. What that often produced was me running headfirst into emotions that were too volatile to deal with constructively, pushing my partners to process with me when they may not have been available, ready or willing to, and trying to sort through emotions that I hadn't even fully examined for myself. I went with whatever my first impulses were, which I later realized weren't always indicative of how I ultimately wanted to respond to my emotions. ❧ Difficult emotions can feel like they need to be addressed right away but it can be beneficial to take a pause, calm down and try to re-center yourself. Examine what is coming up so you can address the emotions from a more informed, clear, calm space, both for yourself and for your partners.

Do you struggle with feeling like difficult emotions have to be dealt with right away? What are some ways you can calm the feeling of urgency when you're in a heightened emotional state?

It is normal to sometimes feel intimidated by the other people your partners are connected to, especially when those people spark our individual insecurities. Breathe, don't judge yourself and remember that even the most amazing human beings are still human.

I once got the opportunity to meet a person who was significant to one of my partners. They were an incredible person. Before I met them, when my partner shared with me who they were, I was excited about being connected to them, but also a little intimidated about who they are. It was mild and didn't knock me off my center, but I still acknowledged it was there and talked to my partner about it. We had a wonderful and reassuring conversation, and I came to the understanding that this person and I both have value to my partner. I don't need to be them and they don't need to be me. ❧ When our partners are connecting to others, it can sometimes cause us to second-guess our own awesomeness, especially when those people hit on insecurities we have about ourselves. It's important to remember that there are many ways to be special and extraordinary. It's also important to remember that even the most incredible of human beings are still human, with their own quirks and insecurities and ordinary states. ❧ Your partner chooses extraordinary people to connect to, and they chose you, right? Because you are extraordinary too.

What are some things you find intimidating when your partners are connecting to other people?

You don't "become" nonmonogamous with one decision to be nonmonogamous. It is a process and a succession of choices.

Just because you have decided to be nonmonogamous, doesn't mean that decision comes with all the tools you need to navigate it successfully. You must still learn, grow, make mistakes and change. The decision is just the beginning of the journey to becoming nonmonogamous. ❦ Choose to think differently. Learn different tools for communicating. Update how you feel about love and relationships. Unpack ways you learned to operate in relationships that don't support being nonmonogamous. Make different relationship choices. Partner with people who support your vision of nonmonogamy. Learn from your mistakes and be accountable. Get in touch with what you really want. It would be lovely if you could make the choice to live this way and everything fell into place around it, but life doesn't really work like that. ❦ It's a constant choice to grow, to embrace, to expand, to learn, to move forward, to become.

What are some ways you have had to "unlearn" monogamy in order to embrace nonmonogamy?

Day 13

It is possible to acknowledge that no one in a situation did anything wrong and still experience uncomfortable emotions about the decisions that were made.

I find this to be one of the most challenging parts of non-monogamy. I have often found myself in situations where I can acknowledge that my partners or my metamours did nothing wrong and yet still struggle with something that happened. When we experience uncomfortable feelings, we often have the impulse to make someone "wrong"—either the other people involved, for something they did, or ourselves for struggling with it. ❧ It is also hard when partners are struggling with your actions, even if you did nothing wrong. You may feel guilt at causing your partner discomfort or have difficult feelings about owning your right to make the choice you made. And these emotions can make it difficult to be compassionate to your partner's feelings—perhaps you worry that doing so means an admission of wrongdoing on your part, or you simply don't understand why your partner is feeling a way about something you were in your right to do. ❧ Truthfully, there's room for both. It can be true both that no one was wrong and that someone experienced discomfort. It is possible to hold both and to have understanding and compassion for both.

When a situation you have experienced brings up difficult emotions for you, do you tend to see your partners or yourself as "in the wrong"? Why?

Day 14

You get to decide what you do and don't want to do and with whom, and your partners also get to have their feelings about those choices.

From sex, to kink, to hobbies, to certain kinds of affection, in nonmonogamous relationships, you might find that you want to interact in certain ways with a particular partner and may not want to interact in the same ways with another. And that's OK. You get to decide what you want to do and with whom. That doesn't mean, however, that those choices won't have any effect on your partners, especially if the things you are doing with others are things they want you to do with them. ❧ You're not wrong for making those choices and your partners aren't wrong for struggling with them. Their work is understanding and accepting your freedom and working through any sense of entitlement they may feel. Your work is having compassion for them as they navigate their hurt and disappointment and working through any guilt you may have around feeling like you must provide something for your partner that you don't wish to. There's room for both. ❧ Make your choices and hold firm to your decisions, but do so with compassion, grace and empathy.

Do you struggle with feeling rejected when your partners choose to do things with others that they don't do with you? Do you struggle with guilt when you engage with some partners in ways you don't with other partners? Why or why not?

Day 15

People who are special to us can spend time with other people who are special to them. It doesn't mean they have forgotten about us or that their heart is far from us.

I was seeing a new person who I really liked. One of their partners had come into town and consequently, they weren't as available to me as I was accustomed to. I was at peace with that because I wanted them to enjoy their connection to the other people in their life and I wanted them to feel free to do that. However, this didn't mean that I didn't feel their absence. I reflected on this and I took a moment to recognize their care for me. Their love for me wasn't absent just because they were with someone else. Their heart wasn't far from me even as they were sharing it with another person. ❧ In the past, I have struggled with this. I would feel forgotten about or like the tie that bound me to a person was somehow severed in the moments they were with another. I wanted to tether people tightly to me and didn't create a lot of room for them to feel free in their love for me. Taking a moment to feel the connection in my heart while also feeling the expanse of the freeness I wished to hold this person in was deeply healing.

Do you take time to feel the love your partners have for you even when they are with others? Is it harder for you to feel it when they are with others? If so, why?

Consider a phrase that we don't use enough in difficult conversations, but that would be helpful: "Hey, what you said hurt me. I don't think that's what you're trying to do. Can you rephrase what you said to still convey your message but be more kind?"

When I'm upset, I can be very sharp. My intent is rarely to hurt the person I'm talking to, but that doesn't mean that what I say isn't hurtful. I have often asked my partners to stop me and let me know if I say something particularly piercing so that I can pause, center myself and think about my word choices because I'm likely communicating from pain. ✻ It isn't easy, but try taking a step back from the words you heard to see that your partner may be struggling to communicate through their pain and let them know that you want to hear them but it's hard for you to do so if they are being hurtful. It can help them to reconsider their word choices moving forward. Give your partners the benefit of the doubt that they aren't trying to hurt you. ✻ Note that this isn't referring to blatant verbal abuse where someone is being unnecessarily cruel and disrespectful. When that is the case, remove yourself entirely from the conversation. You deserve to be spoken to in a respectful and loving manner, even when someone is upset with you.

What reactions do you have when your partner says something hurtful? When your partner makes you aware that you said something hurtful to them, what is your initial response?

Communicating the facts about a situation doesn't automatically communicate how you're feeling about it, and your partners can't respond to your feelings if they don't know what your feelings are.

Your partner tells you they are going on a date on Friday after having gone on a date on Tuesday. You angrily respond to them by saying, "You're going on another date? You already went on one this week!" Those are the facts. ❧ What you didn't say is, "I'm upset that you're going on another date because we haven't been on a date or spent much quality time together in the past week and that's causing me to feel sad and worried that you don't want to spend time with me. I'm concerned that we're becoming disconnected from each other. I'm feeling hurt because I'm worried that I'm not important to you anymore. I'm afraid you don't want to be with me." Those are your feelings. ❧ Assuming that we are communicating our feelings when we are just communicating the facts causes a lot of misunderstanding. You can wind up feeling dismissed because they may not have responded with the empathy you needed, and they can wind up feeling confused because they were simply responding to what you said. Yes, it's more difficult and vulnerable to go deeper and communicate your feelings, but it's the only way for your partners to know what is going on internally with you and respond to that directly.

Do you think that you're communicating your feelings but realize that you are instead communicating your thoughts and observations? What is the distinction?

Day 18

When our partners are in an activated attachment wound state or an activated trauma state, it can be hard for them to clearly state their needs. This is why attunement in our relationships is so important.

Say someone gets hit in the face and their nose is broken. If you run up to them and ask what they need, it's highly likely they won't be able to tell you. They will be in pain, bleeding and disoriented, and won't be centered enough to communicate or even know what they need. ❧ Similarly, when our partners are dealing with a particularly difficult emotion in nonmonogamy, it can be difficult for them to clearly communicate what they need from you. That doesn't justify poor behavior or give them permission to make you responsible for knowing what they need, but it's important to understand that in challenging situations, people aren't always able to clearly communicate their needs or even identify them. This is where the work of attunement comes in. ❧ No, we aren't supposed to be mind readers, but we should pay attention and make a concerted effort to learn the needs of our partners. Likewise, we should expect the people we are in relationships with to pay attention to us and learn our needs. Balance clear communication and working toward attunement with your partners to know each other's needs. Understand also that the work of attunement must be done for each individual relationship you're in and will be different for each partner.

How do you work on attuning to your partners?
What are some ways they can attune to you?

Day 19

Acknowledge when you see growth from your partners, thank them for their willingness to address their uncomfortable emotions to support your freedom and cheer them on when you see them taking steps to challenge themselves.

This is especially important if you're someone who doesn't struggle as much with nonmonogamy and you're in a relationship with someone who does. Instead of focusing on the ways that your partner isn't "on your level" or struggles more than you do, pay attention to and acknowledge when you see them challenging themselves and growing. Your partner likely already feels bad about their struggles. Receiving acknowledgment and encouragement from you can help them to feel like the hard work they are putting in is worthwhile. ❧ Try saying something as simple as "I appreciate all that I see you doing to grow. I know this isn't easy for you and I'm grateful." It's a caring and loving way to generate more of the behaviors you want to see.

In what ways have your partners grown that you can acknowledge and show appreciation for?

Day 20

We don't get to decide for our partners what they should pardon us for or be willing to work through with us, the impact our actions have had on them or what should or shouldn't be a big deal to them.

Have you ever tried to bring up an issue with someone only to have them tell you you're overreacting, that this isn't something that they would be upset about, or that you should let it go? Isn't it infuriating? ❀ We don't get to decide for our partners what they should or shouldn't have feelings about, the impact of our actions, what they should be willing to put up with from us or how they should think and feel about the choices we make. We get to decide how *we* want to deal with all of that, but we don't get to decide any of this for them. ❀ I hear things like, "I've forgiven my partner for so much, but they can't forgive me for this," or "When they go on an overnight, I keep my uncomfortable feelings to myself and am happy for them, but they don't do the same for me," or "I decided I wanted to go to the event with someone else and now my other partner is upset. I wouldn't be upset about something like this." In these situations, you made your choice and the partners made theirs. You choose for you. They choose for them.

Do you sometimes decide how others should think and feel about what you do? How do you feel when others decide how you should think and feel?

Day 21

Sometimes we can get so worked up about something that we catastrophize a situation way beyond what is occurring. Relax, try to remain present, and reserve your emotional energy by not magnifying the situation.

This used to happen to me often. A partner would share with me about an upcoming date or a new romantic interest and my mind would take off like a bullet. "What if they hit it off, and then they fall in love, and then I have a new metamour, and I have to face all of the ways that makes me uncomfortable, and they get another partner while I'm struggling to find others, and they become more connected to the new person than they are to me and…" I would react to all of the feelings those thoughts would generate, turning something that was simple and innocuous into a major issue and expending a ton of emotional energy on fears that almost never came to pass. After experiencing this several times, I learned to temper my thoughts and manage my emotional responses to what was actually happening in the present. ❧ While it was true that all of the things I was fearing could happen, it was equally as true that *none* of the things I was fearing could happen. It's better to just focus on what is currently going on and meet the situation at hand with a proportionate response.

Do you jump to the worst-case scenario when your partners are interacting with other people? If so, why? What prevents you from considering the best-case scenario?

Your partners shouldn't be your sole source of relationship support. Talk to friends you can trust, other nonmonogamous confidants or a therapist instead.

It's important that we have a well-rounded support system to discuss our relationships with that isn't solely composed of our partners. Since our partners can be the people we feel the greatest sense of intimacy with, it's often easy to share our intimate relationship details with them. But having them be our only source of relationship support can be uncomfortable for them, make them privy to information they may not want to know, cause them to feel conflicting emotions about their metamours or push their boundaries around how much support they are willing to offer about our relationships with others. ❧ Having friends, confidants or professionals to talk to is crucial to not making our partners feel like they have to be this space for us or that they have to engage in conversation about relationships to the degree we want them to with no regard for their desires.

Who is in your support network of people you can trust to discuss your relationships with besides your partners?

Day 23

Showing up to love and relationships fully can be scary when you have been hurt in the past. Remind yourself that you are interacting with different people than the ones who hurt you in the past and that you are a different person now. Move in courage.

This is something I consider as I move forward in new relationships. Something will remind me of an old hurt from a former relationship and I'll want to shut things down or run away. To handle this, I say to myself, "This is a different situation, a different person, and *you* are a different person. You are wiser and more aware, and you can make different choices than you did before." ❀ I tell myself that love wasn't the problem—it never is. Rather, the people I chose and the decisions I made in the past weren't right for me or them. I didn't honor my needs or pay attention to our incompatibilities because I wanted to be with them. I remind myself of the ways I've grown as a person and tell myself to trust again, trust others and trust *myself*. ❀ I don't want to show up to new people and new love from a place of hurt, keeping myself reserved and fearful lest I be hurt again. I want to be loved fully, and in order to receive full love, I must give it. I feel the fear and do it anyway. I choose courage. Loving someone is a courageous act. Be brave.

Do you approach love courageously? What ways do you approach love from a place of fear?

If your partner needs to process an issue with you, refrain from using that moment to bring up issues from the past.

Imagine that you and two of your partners go to a party together. After attending the event, one of your partners tells you they felt a little jealous because you paid more attention and showed more affection for your other partner than you did for them, and they ask you to be more mindful of that at future events. ❧ You get defensive and respond to your partner by saying, "Well, two months ago, we went to the beach with you and your partner, and I felt like you paid less attention to me, but I didn't say anything about it. I kept it to myself and worked through it. You do the same thing." ❧ The thing is, no one told you not to bring that up. You made a choice at the time to process your discomfort internally. Bringing up a past issue you had when your partner is trying to advocate for themselves doesn't demonstrate active listening. It redirects the conversation to you instead of acknowledging them, and it isn't really fair because you made a choice not to say something when you could have. ❧ Try to bring up your issues when you have them or initiate a separate conversation to focus on your concerns.

In what ways do you struggle with active listening when partners are communicating their concerns? Do you bring up your own issues when they are trying to address theirs?

Relationships aren't just about how well you get along with someone when you like one another, but also about how well you get along with someone when you're struggling to like one another.

Conflict in relationships is unavoidable and therefore a person's conflict style is an important consideration when partnering with folks. What kind of language do they use when they're upset? How do they hold space for your experience of the conflict? How do they manage their emotions when they are upset? How aware are they of themselves and how accountable are they for their actions and reactions? These are all things we need to pay attention to. Sometimes, we can enjoy a person immensely when we're getting along with them, but really struggle with how they show up to us in conflict because their conflict style is too triggering for us or because they engage in behaviors we want no part of. ❧ If we continue in relationships with partners whose conflict style we don't like, we often try to avoid conflict at all costs, and that isn't sustainable. Conflict is not only unavoidable but also necessary. In conflict, we learn about each other's vulnerabilities, have the hard conversations and experience relationship depth and growth. If your conflict style with a person is incompatible, it will be difficult to achieve this growth.

What things do you notice about yourself when you are in conflict with someone?

No matter what types of relationships we are in, we should be able to say that all of them enable us to maintain our integrity for the kind of person we want to be.

Throughout the course of my being nonmonogamous, I have engaged in various kinds of relationships, from long-term partnerships to casual relationships. In all of them, I make sure I can say that I am maintaining my personal integrity. ❈ If it is a struggle to operate in integrity, that might mean that the partner isn't a good fit for me. If I find myself acting out in anger, being suspicious and cynical or wanting to engage in controlling or limiting behavior, I check in with myself to see if the person allows me to feel safe and that I am able to be my most centered core self. This is not to say that they are responsible for my reactions, but that it's possible we simply aren't fully compatible. ❈ I want to be in relationships in which I can say that I like who I am when I'm with the person. Some people bring out the best in us and others, the worst. They're not bad people—they're just not right for us. Be with people you can be your best version of yourself with.

What does integrity to yourself mean for you
in the context of your relationships?

You do not need to adjust your boundaries because a person you care about is expressing discomfort or difficulty navigating them.

Say you decide that you want to have limited or no interaction with your metamours. Your partner has an event coming up that they'd like you and your metamour to attend. They complain to you about how challenging it is that you don't want to share space with their other partner and that it's making it difficult for them to know who to invite. They remark that they wish you would be around their partner. You can empathize with that being difficult for them and make suggestions around how they can simplify the choice of who to invite, but you do not have to concede your boundary by saying you will go to the event with the metamour, especially if you really don't want to. ❧ Our boundaries are about what *we* need to feel safe, and we don't have to give up pieces of our sense of safety to others because we care about them or because they want us to. It is possible to say, "I understand that this is difficult for you to navigate and I am empathetic to your struggle with this, but this is something *I* need and my upholding of this boundary isn't a lack of care for you but an act of care for me."

In what ways do you feel pressure to adjust your boundaries when the people in your life struggle to navigate them?

Day 28

Constantly questioning your partners' choice of you can feel insulting to your partners. It says that you don't believe what they say and that you don't believe they make good choices about who to give their time to. Believe that they value you.

A friend once mentioned a former partner who constantly questioned why my friend was with them. My friend said that it hurt to repeatedly have their regard for the person questioned and that it felt like their partner was insulting their judgment, as if they couldn't make wise choices about who to be with. ❧ It's OK to be insecure at times. We all need reassurance. And if you have any kind of trauma and/or marginalization, it can be even harder to believe people when they say they value you. However, it is important that we work on believing that we are worthy of the people we are in relationships with and that when they tell us they choose us, it's real. Constantly questioning someone about why they are with you or outright telling them there must be something wrong with them for wanting you can feel hurtful and insulting. ❧ You don't have to magically become secure overnight. Hell, I'm not even there. But try rephrasing your doubts as something like "I struggle to understand the value you see in me, but I appreciate that you do and I'm working on trusting in your regard for me and seeing myself as valuable, too."

What barriers do you face in believing that your partners genuinely value you? How do you find yourself questioning what they see in you or why they are with you?

Day 29

Perpetually fearing that a relationship will end uses mental and emotional energy to exist in a reality that you don't want and takes you away from the relationship that you're in here and now.

One of the affirmations I have created for myself is "Don't waste present-moment energy on a phantom-future scenario." ❧ We often fear the future. What if my partner leaves me to be monogamous with someone else? What if my partner meets someone who is "better" than I am? What if my partner can't handle that sometimes I get jealous, and they break up with me because I'm just too insecure? All these fears about the future are valid, but do you ever stop and ask yourself what is happening right now? ❧ I'm not saying there won't ever come a day where any of these things come to pass—I can't predict the future of your relationships any more than I can predict the future of mine. But if that isn't what is happening right now, why use your present energy on a relationship reality that *isn't* happening? You are present in the reality you don't want and are not engaged in the relationship you currently have. Sometimes we can even bring about the reality we don't want by not being mindful of this. ❧ Be present with the relationship reality you have and don't let fear make you squander it.

What ways does fear affect your ability to remain present in your relationships?

When we are in the throes of jealousy, we can often be so wrapped up in our own experience that we don't stop to consider that our partners have their own feelings and that it's likely difficult for them to navigate our jealousy with us.

Jealousy can be such a visceral emotion. I used to feel it in my gut like I got socked in the stomach, and I'd become emotionally disoriented. When that happened, most of my focus would be on myself and I would give little to no consideration to what my partner was experiencing. Why would I need to think about *them*? They were the one who did the thing that resulted in me feeling jealous, so all the care and consideration should go to me, right? ❀ In truth, my partners often had uncomfortable emotions when I was feeling jealous. They would be anxious that my jealousy would cause me to like them less or worried that I wouldn't be able to handle it and would end my relationship with them. They would feel sad they couldn't connect with me peacefully because of it, guilty or worried that they may have done something wrong or scared that I may not be able to love them as they love others. ❀ It helps me to remember that my emotions aren't the only ones on the stage. Remembering to also have compassion and empathy for my partners helps me to consider how I communicate, behave and care for them even as I am struggling.

How have you noticed your jealousy impact the emotions of your partners?

Learning and being mindful of what our partners are sensitive or insecure about can aid us in having an awareness of the ways our decisions impact them and help us to offer them direct reassurance and support.

"My partner's insecurities are none of my business, nor are they my responsibility." Sound familiar? This is something you might hear often in nonmonogamous discourse. We can debate whether or not this is true or healthy or right with no firm answer—different individuals will have different feelings about this philosophy. ❀ Personally, I tend to fall in the middle. No, my partner's insecurities and sensitivities aren't my responsibility, but I want to be aware of what the difficult areas of polyamory are for them. This helps me to be mindful of the specific ways my actions may affect them and allows me to offer care that feels tailored to them. I am still going to make the choices that feel best for me, but with care to them. ❀ Each partner will have different considerations. One may be sensitive around your newer relationships, while another may feel more insecure around your long-standing partnerships. One may be affected by something that another is indifferent to. It's important to learn what each individual partner feels tender about. ❀ It's also OK if you prefer not to learn about your partners' sensitivities, but if that's your preference, consider aligning with others who also don't wish to do this so you have that understanding of each other.

What sensitivities in nonmonogamy have you shared with your partners and what sensitivities have they shared with you?

Day 32

Supporting a partner through a breakup can be difficult because we often personalize their pain, thinking that if they were happy with us, they wouldn't be sad about losing another. Remember that your partner can love you and still feel grief about their loss.

One of the things I find most interesting about nonmonogamy is that we can often find ourselves and our partners in a variety of relationship environments simultaneously. For instance, I'm currently going through a divorce after 17 years of marriage, shifting from intense new-relationship energy to establishing what commitment and longevity look like for us with my current partner after almost two years of being together and also enjoying a new relationship with another partner. ❀ Sometimes, I get sad about my marriage ending even though I have relationships with folks that I am really excited about and that bring me joy. The people I am engaging with are wonderful, but I still experience periods of grief or loss for my former partner. I appreciate having my partners in my life while feeling sadness for what once was. ❀ Supporting your partners through a breakup means understanding that their sadness has nothing to do with you and you can't "take it away" by being amazing. They get to grieve the loss of someone they cared about, and it doesn't mean that they don't love or care about you. They are hurt and what they need most is for you to love them in that place.

How do you support your partners through breakups? How do you want your partners to support you during a breakup?

Day 33

Sometimes, even with the proper tools, all the reassurance and support from our partners and a grasp on all the necessary logic, we still can't seem to get rid of our uncomfortable feelings. That's OK—sometimes, you just have to feel them.

There have been occasions when I have offered advice on how to deal with a difficult emotion in nonmonogamy and the person has responded by saying, "So what happens if I do that and I still feel bad?" My response is always, "You simply feel it." ❧ I know that's hard to hear. The uncomfortable feelings can be so visceral and persistent that we scramble for *anything* we can do to make them go away. While there will be times when we are able to find ways to alleviate our discomforts more easily, there will also be times when no matter what we do, we just can't shake the feelings. ❧ It is in those moments where we learn to sit with ourselves and our emotions and simply feel them. We learn that we don't always have to *do* something about them. We learn that we can get through feeling uncomfortable and still show up with integrity. We learn that this too shall pass.

Is sitting with your difficult emotions challenging for you? What ways can you encourage yourself to simply feel what you are feeling?

Learning to be present in each of our relationships is a cultivated skill in nonmonogamy. Our partners feel more secure when they see that we can have multiple important relationships but still be present with them.

Learning to be present with the partner in front of us is important to our partners feeling secure in their relationship with us and secure about us having relationships with others. If we are with one partner but our focus is divided, they can usually sense that and it can make them feel like they aren't special to us or that we aren't capable of being with others and still meeting their attention needs. ❧ While I agree that what happens in one relationship can affect what happens in our other relationships, it's important to learn how to disengage from what is happening in our other relationships and plug in to what is happening with the person we are currently with. This means that even if we're having a difficult time in one relationship, we can set that aside and enjoy our other relationships. Similarly, if we have a relationship that is intense and exciting, we're also able to set that aside to enjoy the different energy of our other relationships. ❧ One of the greatest gifts we can give our partners in nonmonogamy is our presence.

What helps you feel like your partners are being present with you? How do you show your partners that you are present with them?

You can't berate, shame, insult or beat yourself up into being "better" at polyamory.

Imagine you are a kid in a classroom and after you get something wrong on an assignment, your teacher says to you, "You are terrible at this and should just give up because you suck." How do you think you'd feel about yourself and your ability to learn the material after that? Probably not that great, right? So why do we do this to ourselves? ❦ We somehow believe that beating ourselves up about our "shortcomings" in nonmonogamy will result in us becoming "better" at it. We aren't kind or encouraging to ourselves, but we think we'll be able to grow despite such harsh treatment of ourselves. It doesn't work that way. ❦ Polyamory brings our inner-child wounds forward and puts us right in contact with our "baby" selves. If you wouldn't berate a child for needing to learn and grow, why would you berate your child-self for the need to do the same? Speak words of grace, love and encouragement to yourself and watch how you blossom.

Do you beat yourself up when you fall short of your expectations for yourself? How do you struggle to offer yourself compassion and grace?

You can feel compersion simultaneously with jealousy or envy. They don't always cancel each other out, and the presence of one doesn't invalidate the other.

I once had the opportunity to attend a rope class with my partner and my metamour. I was positively elated watching them practice the ties and watching my partner bottom to my meta. They have such a beautiful relationship and I enjoy watching them together very much because I love them both so dearly. I took pictures and laughed with them. It was so special. ❀ However, there was a moment when they were sitting together listening to the facilitator talk about the next week's class that I felt a pang of envy. Since I live across the country from my partner, we can't attend a weekly class or regular event together, and that made me feel a little sad. And yet, all the compersion and beauty I felt from being in the class with them was still very much present alongside my envy. I took a moment to just marvel at the human heart and all it can hold at once. ❀ Compersion isn't the opposite of jealousy to me. Rather, it's a separate emotion that can be felt in addition to jealousy, envy, insecurity or a variety of uncomfortable emotions. To me, it's important to be present for everything that we are feeling, not choose one emotion as more favorable than another. They are all valid and all important.

Do you experience compersion and jealousy alongside each other? How does it affect you when both emotions are present?

Often, when we have difficult emotions about something our partners are doing with someone else, we communicate our feelings using accusatory language that implies or directly says that our partners are wrong for doing something that made us uncomfortable. Mind your words.

This is the difference between saying, "When you spend the weekend with your other partner, you don't text me. I get sad about that because I miss you and I think you don't miss me or that you forget about me," and saying, "You just go away with them and completely forget about me! I don't hear from you at all!" Both essentially say the same thing, but which do you think will receive a more compassionate response? ❀ It's hard for our partners to get close to what we are trying to say if they are dodging accusations in our message. If they didn't do anything wrong, it's important to acknowledge that, even if their actions caused you discomfort. Using language that allows room for both of those things to be true allows for you both to be represented in the conversation. If your partners don't feel accused of wrongdoing, they will be more inclined to hear you out and offer support. ❀ Take time to develop how you communicate your emotions so that you are honoring both your partners' autonomy and your emotional autonomy. Remember, it's not you against them. It's you together, trying to care for each other.

How can you be more intentional about the language you use when communicating difficult emotions to your partners?

Our partner wanting something different in another relationship doesn't make the other person "better" than us or mean that our partner values them more. Usually, it simply means the other person is more available or more compatible for what our partner wants.

In nonmonogamy, we can find ourselves dealing with partners who choose to marry, nest, parent, go into business or do something else that feels significant with people other than us, and that can challenge our sense of our worth. It's easy to make it about us lacking in some way, even if we never wanted those things with our partner. It can be hard to not personalize their decision and to see it from their perspective. The reality is that their action is likely them choosing the person they feel safest and most confident with for that project. They're choosing the person they feel is most compatible with them for that desire. More often than not, it isn't a statement of their lack of love or regard for us. ❦ This can be difficult to reconcile, and that's OK. You can recognize that your partner did nothing wrong in choosing someone they felt was best for that thing, and simultaneously acknowledge that it hurts that they didn't choose you. Similarly, if you are the partner who decided to pursue an action with someone and your other partner is struggling with it, have compassion and empathy.

Do you feel hurt or rejected when your partners choose others for different relationship experiences than they choose with you? How do you address this with yourself and your partners?

Day 39

It is possible to feel jealousy and still respond in ways that are in alignment with the goals you've set for yourself and who you want to be in nonmonogamy.

Before when I felt jealousy, I immediately reacted in the way it was prompting me to. My initial impulses to become angry, sullen, withdrawn and insecure were the only options I thought I had available to me as responses to experiencing that emotion. With time and work and practice, I now know that I can feel jealous but not act from a place of jealousy. I ask myself if the feelings I'm experiencing support how I want to show up overall and I make different choices. ❧ And this isn't about "faking" that I'm OK when I'm not or pretending I have different feelings. That's inauthentic. It's saying, "Yeah, sometimes the choices that people make will trigger my jealousy but what I ultimately want is for folks to feel free and supported with me and I can do that even when my emotions aren't completely on board."

What are some of the impulses you have when you are feeling jealous? Do they align with how you wish to behave overall?

Having uncomfortable feelings about what my partners are doing with others doesn't mean I don't want them to do those things. I want my partners to have the freedom to authentically pursue their happiness.

I'm an external emotional processor and I like to process my emotions (within reason) with my partners. I am a person who experiences jealousy, envy and other uncomfortable emotions in nonmonogamy, and it can be challenging sharing that with my partners. They can sometimes interpret my discomforts as me not wanting them to do whatever it is I'm feeling uncomfortable about. ❧ While I recognize that people often share their emotions with the intention of getting their partners to stop or change what they are doing (or to be emotionally manipulative), for me, I just need to be heard and understood. If I have a specific request to make of my partner for support, I ask for that directly. I want to support their freedom. I'm just wading through complicated feelings to do so. Unless I directly say, "I don't want you to do that thing," that's not what I'm saying. ❧ Polyamory is a marvel to me in that you can simultaneously feel supportive of your partners' freedom *and* feel your own discomfort.

Do you sometimes interpret your partners having difficult emotions about your choices as them wanting you to change those choices?

Remember that love can be expressed differently in each individual relationship without those differences of expression meaning that one person is loved more than another.

My first polyamorous relationship was a triad. Once, on one partner's birthday, my other partner and I made online birthday posts for them, and our partner responded one way to mine and a different way to the other partner's. I felt slighted by this, and I was kind of a pill about it. On their birthday to boot! It was not my finest moment. ❧ As I was leaving for work that day, I kissed my son once on the forehead and hugged him. Then I kissed my daughter several times and hugged her. A light came on. I used different expressions of love for each child but it didn't mean that I loved my daughter more than my son. That's just what came out at that time. ❧ Different expressions of love do not always mean one person is loved more than another. And truthfully, while I want the quality of love I receive from the people in my life to be the same, I don't want them to love me in the exact same ways they do others because that wouldn't account for who I am and how I personally want and need to be loved. The love we share should be unique and personal to each other.

Do you sometimes compare how your partners express love for others to how they express love for you? How does it make you feel if you do?

It takes humility to share the love and care of our partners with other people. Embrace that you are not the sole source, or always the best source, to meet their wants and needs, and understand that that's OK.

One of my favorite books is *Loving What Is* by Byron Katie. In it, there's a quote that reads something like, "to assume that you know what's best for a person, even when it's coming from a place of love, is pure arrogance." It stuck with me. ❀ It is a deeply humbling experience learning to accept and embrace that you are not all a person wants and needs to be fulfilled. As a partner, a parent, a friend, even as an employee, we can't be everything to the people in our lives. Sharing the space of caring for our loved ones with others requires humility. It requires understanding that other people can sometimes provide for our loved ones what we can't. It requires believing that our loved ones know best what they want and need and with whom. It requires putting our egos to the side and collaborating with others so our loved ones can truly be well. It requires remembering that it's not about us.

How has polyamory encouraged a deeper sense of humility in you?

Our emotions tell us the truth about how we feel, but they don't always tell us the truth about what is happening. Remembering this helps us to honor their message, but not allow that message to completely shape our perception of reality.

Emotions are useful for alerting us to what our inner experience is of our external reality, but they aren't always the most accurate gauge for what is actually happening. You may feel sad because you think your partner forgets about you when they are with another person, but that doesn't mean they actually do forget about you. ❀ Learn how to hold space for what your emotions are telling you while understanding that it may not be a concrete reflection of reality. This helps us to not judge our emotions harshly or dismiss them while also not allowing them to completely dictate our perception of what is happening. We can honor our emotions and also try to see the entire picture, not just what is reflected through our lens.

Do you often get caught up in believing that the story your emotions are telling you is the truth about what is happening? What are some ways you ground yourself back to reality?

While challenging ourselves with new experiences in nonmonogamy is important for growth, it's OK to say no to things you don't feel ready for or don't want to engage in.

Once, I asked a former partner when I was going to meet a new person he had been seeing for a few months. He told me that when he brought it up to her, she confessed that she had too much anxiety about meeting me and wasn't ready. That initially irritated me because I perceived her decision as her trying to act like I didn't exist or not respecting my place in his life. But after some reflection, I realized we didn't have to meet, especially if she felt it would be harmful for her, and us not meeting each other had no effect on either of our relationships with him. I let it go. ❧ Often, folks will push themselves to engage in situations that they aren't ready for simply to appear "better" at polyamory. While that can sometimes yield surprisingly positive results, more often than not, pushing ourselves to do things we aren't ready for causes discomfort at best and damage at worst. This isn't to say that you should never challenge yourself, but take care in how and when you choose to do so. It's OK to acknowledge to yourself and your partners that you aren't ready or willing to do something you feel will be more harmful than helpful for you.

Have you ever pushed yourself to do something in polyamory that you weren't ready for in order to appear "polyam perfect"? How did that work out?

Day 45

Our partners expressing joy and excitement about others doesn't mean they no longer feel joy or excitement about us or that their appreciation of someone else diminishes their appreciation for us.

Earlier in my journey, I didn't encourage my partners to share much about their relationships with others. Outside of basic information for transparency and practicality, I didn't want to hear much about my partners' other connections and certainly didn't want to hear them gushing about someone else. It would activate feelings of jealousy, envy and insecurity, and I would worry about whether I was now less appealing to my partner. It's OK if this is how you feel too. ✿ Those feelings still occasionally come up when my partners share their excitement about others, but less so as I've come to understand this concept: They can be excited about them *and* excited about me. It's not an either/or situation. I can hold space for that excitement without feeling lesser or like my relationship with my partner is jeopardized by their enjoyment of another. ✿ I also want to point out that it is much easier for our partners to be at ease with our excitement about someone else when we make sure to still express excitement about them.

How can your partners express to you that they are excited about their relationship with you? How do you express excitement for your partners?

When you are overly concerned about not hurting your partners' or metamours' feelings, you can end up sacrificing your own feelings. Understand that even with the best intentions, hurt feelings will happen and acknowledge the impact of your choices when they do.

In nonmonogamy, I often find that people are either so concerned about the feelings of others that they neglect their own feelings or that they put their own feelings first and are unconcerned about the feelings of others. There should be a balance that allows us to care for the feelings of others while also caring for our own. ❧ Considering our partners' feelings or the feelings of our metamours is important, but not to the point that we don't consider our own feelings. Also, hurt feelings are unavoidable in this journey. Rather than going through emotional gymnastics trying to keep everyone from being hurt, do the best you can to be a considerate person and then do the best you can to be a supportive person when, inevitably, someone's feelings get hurt. Trying to anticipate everything that may cause your partner pain and seeking to eliminate those occurrences removes opportunities for them to grow from the challenges. Trust that they can manage their emotions and take care of your own.

Do you find yourself prioritizing the feelings of others above your own feelings? What happens when you do?

It's OK to not know how to regulate yourself when your attachment fears and traumas get activated by polyamory, especially in the beginning stages. These skills take time and work to develop.

Sometimes, I encounter clients who are fresh from experiencing a challenge in nonmonogamy that they didn't respond well to or how they would have liked to. They are often disappointed in themselves and can't understand why they couldn't figure out how to "pull themselves together." And many times, these folks are new to polyamory. ❀ My response is usually, "Why would you know?" This is all new terrain. These are all new emotional experiences. Nonmonogamy triggers our attachment fears and traumas in ways we have likely never experienced before. Even after a decade of nonmonogamy, I still experience new challenges. ❀ Give yourself some grace and compassion. Understand that you have to learn new ways to self-regulate your emotions around these new experiences. Don't judge yourself too harshly when you don't know how to do that and fumble through. ❀ This doesn't negate the fact that you *do* need to develop polyamory-specific tools to regulate your emotions, and it doesn't excuse you from accountability for your actions when in an activated state. There are plenty of tools available to help you learn the skills you need. Seek out support from other polyamorous folks, online resources, books about attachment in nonmonogamy (such as Jessica Fern's *Polysecure*) or a therapist who is familiar with nonmonogamy.

What skills have you developed to self-regulate in your nonmonogamous journey?

Day 48

Whether a relationship is casual or an established partnership, you should feel empowered to ask for what you need and make your desires clear.

As I date and connect to folks, I am mindful of checking in with myself to see if I feel empowered to communicate my needs to them. Sometimes, when I'm in the early stages of forming a connection with someone, I'll identify a desire or need and I'll grapple with expressing it for fear that it's too soon or that we aren't "there" yet. Then I remind myself that in all my interactions, I want to be able to express my genuine desires and needs. Also, the quickest way to be sure someone can respond well to me stating my needs and wants is by doing exactly that. ❧ We should be in relationships where we feel we can genuinely express what we want and need. The other person may not be able or willing to provide those things for us (and that's OK), but folks should at least be able to hold space for those expressions.

What struggles do you experience around communicating your needs and wants to others?

Learn to appreciate when conflict happens in your relationships. While not enjoyable, conflict is an opportunity to learn about ourselves and our partners, develop resolution skills, build resilience and strengthen our intimacy and vulnerability with others.

My current partner and I have a very peaceful relationship. The few times we have found ourselves in conflict, I always marvel at (and am sometimes bothered by) how calm he remains. I have an anxious attachment style and conflict with a partner can really activate my attachment issues. ❧ He told me that while he doesn't like conflict, he understands that it is inevitable and necessary for us to build a deeper, more meaningful relationship. It's how we learn about each other's sensitivities and needs, how we practice being vulnerable with one another and a way to develop more effective communication. Conflict reminds us that we can experience difficulties in our relationship but still seek to show one another care and love. His perspective has helped me to adjust my own perspective. ❧ Conflict isn't fun. You shouldn't encourage it, and if you have constant conflict with someone, it's likely there's something unhealthy going on. But for healthy partnerships, some conflict isn't bad—it's a vital and necessary part of being in a relationship. Further, some of the difficulties we experience around conflict come not from the conflict itself, but our avoidance of it. Learn to embrace it. Conflict doesn't only produce separation. It can also produce closeness.

Are you conflict avoidant? Do you dread conflict in your relationships so much that you actively avoid addressing things? What scares you about conflict?

Day 50

It takes courage and vulnerability for our partners to share hard truths with us. Telling a loved one something that you know will cause them pain isn't easy. Keep that in mind.

I reflected on this as I was thinking about my marriage ending and how difficult it must have been for my husband to finally tell me he no longer wanted to be with me. In many cases, I believe it's just as hard to break up with a person as it is to be broken up with. ❧ When our partners share things that are difficult to hear or painful, we can sometimes respond in ways that don't encourage honesty. I have definitely been guilty of wanting honesty from my partners, but then not handling their honesty in ways that helped them feel comfortable continuing to be honest with me. ❧ Try to remember that it took courage and vulnerability for your partner to share their truth with you. Have compassion for how difficult it may have been for them to be honest with you, knowing that you might be hurt by what was said. If you can recognize that they did their best to be compassionate in their honesty, be compassionate in your response to it. You may not appreciate what was said, but you can appreciate that they had the courage to say it and be real with you.

Do you honor the courage it takes for your partners to share a vulnerable or hard truth with you? How do you show that?

Sometimes, we can "catastrophize" our emotions to ourselves, making them appear larger and more intense than they are. The language we use to communicate our emotions to ourselves is important.

I recall a time when I was thinking about something I had to do and I said to myself, "I'm feeling a lot of angst about this." I then examined that thought and realized that it wasn't accurate. I wasn't actually feeling a lot of angst, but was experiencing a measure of concern, which seemed far more manageable and less disruptive to my emotional state. Just acknowledging that distinction reduced my stress about it. ❧ If I could go back and give my younger self a piece of advice, I would tell myself to avoid making such a big deal out of things that really weren't that big of a deal. I wasted a lot of energy making things into much larger issues than they actually were. ❧ I'm not saying to downplay your emotions — that causes other problems, especially in cases of abuse or poor treatment. There are definitely times when the depth of your emotions is appropriate to what is happening and you need to acknowledge that. I'm saying to examine what you're feeling and check to see if what you're communicating to yourself is accurate. Taking the time to examine what is going on decreases the likelihood that you'll have exaggerated responses to your emotions and helps you to respond in an appropriate manner.

Do you often find that you exaggerate your emotions to yourself? Do you minimize your emotions to yourself? How can you accurately assess your emotional state?

Your partners can't make promises for their future selves. They can't promise you that the relationship will never change, that they'll never change or that their feelings will never change. And you can't make any of those promises to them, either.

I recall being on the bus listening to "Gone Away" by H.E.R. There's a lyric in the song that says, "You promised you wouldn't change. It'd stay the same. But it's different." I thought that, realistically, no one can promise that a relationship will stay the same, or that they will. ❀ Our partners can't promise that they are always going to want to remain married, or nested, or maintain a hierarchy or stay poly-fidelitous. They can't guarantee that they will continue in a sexual and/or romantic relationship with us, or that they will desire us in the same way they did when they embarked on their relationship with us. People change, feelings change, needs change. The same thing is true for us. We change, our feelings change, our needs change. Sometimes our relationships can weather those changes, but sometimes they can't. Holding on too rigidly to people and their feelings staying exactly the same or our relationships with them never changing makes acceptance much harder when those changes inevitably occur. ❀ Folks are allowed to and *will* change. And you will, too. Make your peace with this.

> Does the thought of yourself or your partners changing cause fear or anxiety for you? What about them changing is scariest for you?

It is not possible to get all the reassurance we need, whenever we need it, from our relationships. We have to learn to provide ourselves with the reassurance that we need to feel safe and secure.

While I believe that we should be in relationships with people who enthusiastically and freely show up to reassure us, it is impossible for someone to be the sole source of all the reassurance we need whenever and however we need it. If I had a partner who responded to my reasonable needs for reassurance with resistance and judgment, they wouldn't remain a partner for very long. But even from a practical standpoint, you may find yourself seeking reassurance and your partner isn't available because they are with another partner, at work or going through their own emotional process. ❧ It's important that you're able to provide your own sense of security when you're feeling insecure or vulnerable and that you don't seek reassurance exclusively from partners. Ideally, there should be a balance of your partners providing reassurance and you developing the tools to offer reassurance to yourself. It's a both/and situation.

How do you offer reassurance to yourself?

When we make a mistake in polyamory or fall short of our standards for ourselves, we can begin to think we are too much of a "mess" for nonmonogamy. Remember that you are not a mess, but a work in progress.

Think of your nonmonogamy like a construction project. Construction sites look messy, with materials and equipment everywhere. It's hard to see how all that mess turns into beautifully crafted buildings. Usually, there are setbacks, timeline changes and revisions in the construction process. ❧ We are no different. We are works in progress. There is no crime in making a mistake, struggling to attain what you set out to do or taking longer than you planned. And even if you sometimes feel like a mess, remember that messes can always be cleaned up. ❧ Maybe you are struggling to manage jealousy or working through your need to feel "first." Perhaps you had every intention of getting through your partner's weekend away with a love without crying but a picture of the two of them together set you off and you feel like a failure. You're not. You're a human being who is building something new within yourself. Have grace. Have hope. Have perseverance. Have compassion.

Do you sometimes feel like you are too much of a mess for polyamory, especially in moments where you have fallen short of your standards for yourself? How do you reassure yourself when you are feeling this way?

There's liking a person and then there's liking the relationship you have with them, and sometimes, those are two drastically different things.

Sometimes, no matter how much you like and enjoy spending time with a person, the relationship you can reasonably have with them doesn't serve your needs. It's important to remember that it is not only necessary to appreciate the person you are with but to appreciate what you have *with* them. ❀ It can be difficult to be in a relationship with someone who you very much like but recognize that you don't enjoy your relationship experience with them. When that is the case, you may need to collaborate with them to see if adjustments can be made to the relationship to make it work, or if the relationship needs to end.

Have you ever found yourself in a relationship where you liked the person but didn't like the relationship you had with them? If so, how did you handle it?

Our partners being jealous or envious of our interactions with others can sometimes feel as if they don't want us to have joy or good things. However, the feelings usually aren't personal to us and say more about how they feel about themselves.

In my marriage, I was the one who struggled with jealousy. My husband did not, and it was baffling to me. One evening, I asked him why he never seemed to experience difficult emotions around my interactions with others. His response made me cry. He asked why he would feel badly or be upset about me receiving more love and happiness in my life. He wanted me to have as much love as I could get. ❀ I cried because it helped me to understand why my jealousy and envy was so hurtful to him. It made him feel as if I didn't want him to have joy or pleasure or happiness. That was never the case—I wanted him to have all those things—but him receiving them from others made me feel badly about me. I wanted to be happy for him, but I didn't know how to when I was feeling so bad. My expressions of jealousy often looked like I didn't care about his experience. ❀ Try not to take your partner's jealousy personally. It's usually not about what they don't want you to have—it's not about you at all, really. It's about what is going on inside of them.

Do you take your partner's feelings of jealousy or envy personally? How does their jealousy feel personal to you?

It takes time and self-work for our emotions to catch up to the logic of nonmonogamy. Our logic not matching our emotions doesn't mean that either of them are invalid, and it's OK to allow them both to exist as they are.

"My partner is on a date tonight. I know what they're doing and who they're with. We are in a consensually nonmonogamous relationship. They are doing nothing wrong. So why do I feel so upset about it?" ❧ Sound familiar? I know I've had similar conversations with myself many times on my journey. I had all the logic right there at the front of my mind: we're nonmonogamous, we've agreed to not be exclusive, I'm also interacting with others, what my partners are doing isn't wrong. And yet, the logic did little to assuage my feelings. ❧ I eventually learned that it's OK for your thoughts and your feelings to not always be on the same page. It's OK to apply the logic of nonmonogamy and also acknowledge that your emotions haven't caught up yet or just aren't always going to match it. It's OK to say, "My partner is on a date right now and I know logically, there's nothing wrong but I'm still feeling difficult emotions about it." Our logic can exist alongside contradictory emotions and one doesn't need to cancel out the other.

When your emotions and your logic aren't in alignment with each other, what makes recognizing both as valid hard for you?

We often assume our partners' motivations based on what it would mean if we did that thing. Remember that your partners are different people than you and that they have different motivations than you. Ask for clarity.

One of my favorite quotes by Anaïs Nin is, "We don't see things as they are, we see things as we are." In nonmonogamy, we can get upset at our partners for something because we assume it means that they care more about another partner than they do us, that they are losing their desire and value for us or that they are more interested in someone else than in us. This often happens because that's what the thing in question would mean to us if *we* did it. When we're upset, we can connect our partners' motivations to our biggest fears and insecurities, looking for confirmation of what we secretly believe is going on. ❧ Before you assume a particular motivation is influencing your partners' actions and get upset, ask them what was behind the choice that they made. You will gain an understanding of how your partner thinks and you will likely be surprised by the answer, possibly finding that it had nothing to do with what you originally thought was going on. Give your partners a chance to offer you clarity.

Do you assume the motivations of your partners based on your own motivations? What prevents you from recognizing that they are different people?

Our partners expressing discomfort about something we are doing isn't the same as them telling us not to do it. If we decide to change our choice based on their feelings, we can't make them responsible for that.

When a partner expresses difficult or uncomfortable emotions about our choices in nonmonogamy, it is not the same as them saying, "Change your choice" or "Don't do that." It is simply them expressing the emotional impact they're experiencing from what you're doing. People will often change their decisions due to their partner's struggles with their choices and then resent their partner because they "couldn't" do what they wanted. The reality is that they could have done it but chose not to because prioritizing their partner's feelings above their personal desire had more value to them. If you choose to do this, you need to own it. ❀ I also want to acknowledge that some people may have such large reactions to what we are doing that they make navigating nonmonogamy with them exhausting, causing you to feel guilt and like you have no choice but to change what you're doing or deal with a huge fallout. That's not OK. If that is the case, you need to reevaluate if you can continue navigating nonmonogamy with that person.

When your partners express difficult emotions about your choices in polyamory, do you feel as if you need to make changes to your choices, even when they didn't ask for that? Why?

Judging ourselves for our jealousy, discomfort or insecurity in nonmonogamy can impede our ability to deal with these emotions. If we're too caught up in feeling badly, we have less space and energy to face the feelings.

I find that two things happen when we judge ourselves for our emotions: We either spiral into shame and self-loathing because we think we shouldn't feel this way, berating ourselves and thus making ourselves feel worse, or we refuse to acknowledge the feeling because we don't want to see ourselves as someone who has those kinds of emotions. ❀ Either way, the judgment impairs your ability to deal with the feelings. If you're in a space of self-loathing, you have to deal with feeling badly about yourself in addition to the original feelings. Most folks have a hard time accessing their belief in their own efficacy from a space of feeling bad about themselves. And you simply can't do anything about resolving an emotion you won't acknowledge is there. ❀ So ditch the self-judgment. You feel what you feel. Emotions don't make you stupid, childish or a "bad" person—they just make you human. Have compassion for your humanity, love your emotional self and focus on addressing the feelings without harsh judgment so you can make wise choices.

Does self-judgment get in the way of you dealing with your uncomfortable emotions? What are some emotions you judge yourself for having?

It is important to remember to speak *for* our emotions, not *from* them. We should feel our feelings, but not become them.

A former partner and I used to be in an online polyamory group together and he once made a comment on a post remarking how sexy he found it that so many women in the group had multiple college degrees. I do not have a college degree and barely graduated high school. ❋ When I read his comment, I fell apart. I went off on him, cried and even made a passive-aggressive post about it. I didn't even realize until that moment that I had an insecurity about not having a degree and him finding women with degrees more desirable than me. While my insecurity was valid, my behavior was completely unacceptable. ❋ Had I communicated *for* my feelings instead of *from* them, I would have said that I was feeling insecure and afraid he desired women who were college graduates more than he did me. Had I not become my insecurity, I would have asked for reassurance and connection instead of using language that was accusatory and repellant. ❋ We can feel our emotions, but we shouldn't become our emotions. We can speak for them, but we shouldn't let them speak for us. It's important to work on remaining centered in our core selves even in the face of feeling strong emotions so that we can communicate in ways that are in alignment with who we ultimately wish to be.

Have you ever spoken *from* your emotions instead of *for* them? What happens when you become your emotions instead of feeling them?

It takes practice to learn how to compassionately and empathetically sit with a partner experiencing discomfort about something we did but not internalize that as having done something wrong.

Our partners experiencing discomfort about our inter-actions with others doesn't mean that what we did was wrong, and offering them compassion and empathy for that discomfort isn't accepting responsibility for wrongdoing or blame for their emotions. Learning to make that distinction can make all the difference in our relationships. ❀ I often find that folks have a hard time being compassionate and empathetic to their partners when they are struggling because of their own feelings of guilt about their partner being uncomfortable with a choice they made. If you didn't violate an agreement and whatever you did was within your right to do, then you weren't wrong for doing it. Your partner is just having difficult feelings about it, and that's OK too. You can validate that difficulty and still maintain your right to autonomy in your choices. ❀ Even when our partners suggest or accuse us of wrongdoing (intentionally or not), if we are secure in ourselves and what we know is right for us, we can respond to their feelings without accepting their perception of our actions or assuming guilt. It's being able to say, "I know you are uncomfortable with what I did and that's valid, but I wasn't wrong for doing it, even if you feel that way."

When your partners experience discomfort about your nonmonogamy, do you feel as if you've done something wrong? If so, why?

Unless you are someone who naturally experiences compersion, expecting to feel it automatically when shifting from monogamy to nonmonogamy is unrealistic and a lofty goal. Focus on arriving at neutrality first.

When I first became polyamorous, I would see so much mention of compersion as if it was this magical and completely necessary emotion for navigating nonmonogamy. I struggled to feel compersive about my partner's interactions with others and the fact that I couldn't caused me to feel bad at polyamory. ❁ After years of living this way and marginally experiencing compersion, I learned it's not actually necessary for happy and healthy polyamory. I also learned that expecting to experience compersion automatically when you leave monogamy is unrealistic. We live in a society that perpetuates the idea that you should feel horrible about your partner being with someone else. The expectation of jumping from feeling bad about it to feeling good about it skips a huge swath of emotions. ❁ Focus on arriving at neutral first. Look at your partner being with other people as neither bad nor good, but simply reality. Then you can decide if you wish to cultivate compersion or that you don't need it. Personally, I am OK with feeling minimal compersion. I'm happy my partners are living the lives they desire and making choices that contribute to their fulfillment, even if some of those choices cause me some discomfort.

What are your expectations of yourself around compersion? Are you compassionate toward yourself if you don't feel it?

Day 64

Someone rejecting us doesn't mean that we should reject ourselves.

I've dealt with a lot of rejection in my life, and it's never a good feeling. Nonmonogamy has made me confront my relationship with rejection to a heightened degree because I'm interacting more in ways that increase the potential for rejection. ❀ I also find that rejection in non-monogamy is its own unique experience. In monogamy, if someone you're interested in has a partner, you can at least rationalize the rejection without personalizing it. Rejection in nonmonogamy feels more personal to me because you know the person is open to and capable of having relationships with as many folks as they wish to, but you're just not one of those folks. It can be hard not to feel badly about yourself. ❀ I have tried to learn to accept a person's rejection of me in a particular way without turning their rejection inward onto myself. I may not be appealing to them in a romantic or sexual way, but that doesn't mean I'm not appealing. I may not work for them but that doesn't mean I don't work at all. I'm a person who some folks will be into and some folks won't. And I always have the ability to be deeply into myself.

Does experiencing rejection from others cause you to reject yourself? In what ways do you take others' opinion of you onto yourself?

Day 65

While it is important to be honest with our partners about our feelings and experiences with others, be mindful about how you relay that information as it might be challenging for them to hear.

Some folks love hearing their partners gush about their new connections or other partners. I am not one of them. While I enjoy my partners' honesty and am happy when they are enjoying their connections with others, I tend to want that information to be concise. I want my partners to understand that hearing this kind of information may activate uncomfortable feelings, so gushing to me about someone else isn't the best strategy. ❋ It's the difference between saying, "My new partner is the most interesting person I've ever met!" and saying, "I find my new partner incredibly interesting, and I am enjoying getting to know them." It's choosing to say, "I am enjoying our sexual interactions and they are very fulfilling for me" rather than, "Our sexual chemistry is off the charts!" ❋ Be mindful of phrasing things in a way that will be easier for your partner to hear, especially if you have a partner you know struggles with this kind of information, while still being fully honest.

How do you show mindfulness when communicating with your partners about your other interactions with folks? What ways do you need your partners to be mindful of you when they are communicating with you about other people?

If you feel the need to find another relationship in order to be happy with the relationship you are in, chances are that you're just not happy in that relationship and starting another will likely not change that.

My husband was a good person and treated me as well as he could, but in my marriage a lot of my needs went unmet. I clamored after other relationships to find avenues to meet my needs, helping to make accepting the little I got from him OK. ❧ Shortly after I met my current partner, my spouse initiated our separation. I found myself with one partner and a void in my romantic relationship space. I noticed, however, that even though I wasn't happy about the idea of having one partner, I was extremely happy in my relationship. I felt fulfilled and felt less angst to acquire other relationships because the one I had met my most important needs. Since I wasn't "starving" in my relationship, I was able to be patient as I waited on my next love to come along. ❧ If you need something or someone outside of your relationship to help you to be happy with it, it's likely that it's not what you want and need regardless. Placing the happiness of a relationship on people or things outside of it rarely works. There's a difference between wanting other partners to feel fulfilled in your nonmonogamy and wanting other partners to help you cope with the partners you have.

Do you seek other partners to help you cope with your current relationships? How would you feel if someone sought you to help them cope with a relationship?

Avoid entering into relationships with folks who require you to cut off important parts of who you are. You deserve partners who not only accept but celebrate the most authentic and integrated version of you.

I am very cognizant of not entering into relationships that require me to cut off, stifle or limit important versions of myself. ❀ For example, I'm a bisexual woman and I often find that many women in the lesbian community refuse to date bisexual women. Say I met a polyamorous lesbian who was interested in being with me but declared that I would have to agree to stop dating men. No matter how much I liked her and wanted to be with her, I would refuse. That would be asking to cut off an important part of who I am. ❀ Maybe someone wants to be with you but wants you to stop being kinky. Or you are a person of color interacting with a white person who wants you to stop being so vocal about your experiences of white supremacy and racism. Maybe you're a bi/pansexual/ queer person and someone wants you to agree to not date a particular gender or trans individuals. Whatever it is, if someone asks you to not be who you are, they aren't asking to be with you but the version of you they would be most comfortable with. ❀ Relationships work best when we can be our most authentic and integrated version of who we are.

Have you ever been in a relationship where you cut off parts of yourself to remain in it? If so, how did that feel?

Our feelings are always valid, but they may not always be proportionate to the situation.

I personally don't subscribe to the notion that we "should" or "shouldn't" feel anything. We feel what we feel, and those feelings are always valid. We serve them best when we acknowledge their right to exist without judging them or ourselves for having them. However, sometimes feelings are not proportionate to the situation. ❀ Yes, it is valid to feel jealous or upset at something your partner may have done in polyamory but often the level of upset we feel isn't proportionate to the event. For example, being incredibly angry or upset at your partner for going to a restaurant that you wanted to try with someone else before you, when you never even mentioned that you wanted to go there with them in the first place, probably isn't reasonable. ❀ This also works in the other direction. Sometimes, we aren't as upset as we should be about clear boundary violations or clear disregards of our relationship, time or feelings and only recognize it later. This doesn't mean you should go off about it, but perhaps you need to be firmer about expressing that you are not OK with something as it happens. ❀ Learn to honor your genuine feelings while also critically examining the proportion at which they are showing up.

Do you sometimes experience feelings in a way that is on reflection disproportionate to the situation? How do you adjust your feelings when you notice that?

Our partners are allowed to change. They have the right to explore and discover new things and to meet people who introduce them to different ideas and identities. This can feel threatening, but we can't let fear cause us to limit or control another person.

A former partner once told me that he was going to a kink class at a local adult shop the following week. He had a few partners who were into kink and he wanted to see if there was something there for him. I mentally panicked. In my mind, he was going to go to that class, become super kinky and connect with his other loves in a deeper way that would make our connection pale in comparison. He was going to decide that he no longer wanted any vanilla relationships. My mind went from zero to our relationship ending in .25 seconds. We are no longer together, and I think a large issue in our relationship was him not feeling free to develop himself without having to deal with my emotions about it. ❧ Our partners are allowed to change, to discover new versions of themselves and to meet people who open them up to new personal possibilities. Sometimes those changes are scary for us. Sometimes, they even take the person away from us or make it so we can no longer be together. They still get to do it, though. And we're also allowed to change.

When partners begin to shift and change, do you get fearful about the future of your relationship? How can you ask for reassurance when you are afraid of the changes?

It can be difficult for some folks to process their partner's feelings and their own feelings about an issue at the same time.

I'm a very emotional and emotionally connected person and I had a former partner who was not. When we would have issues, they struggled to process my emotions against their own emotions, and even to process their emotions about my emotions. It was challenging because they would get overwhelmed, and I would get frustrated. It felt like they weren't responding to my thoughts and feelings with thoughts and feelings of their own. ❧ A way to address this is scheduling dedicated time to talk about an issue so you and your partner have space to sit with how you feel about it apart from one another. You can also allot a certain period of time during a discussion for each person to have their say while the other actively listens. ❧ If you are the person who struggles to process multiple sets of emotions simultaneously, it can be helpful to know this about yourself and to say to your partner, "I want to respond to this but I'm going to need some time to sit with what I'm feeling apart from what you're feeling to get a gauge on what my experience of this is. Can we set aside time for you to express yourself, me to process what you've said and then time for me to express myself?"

Do you struggle to process multiple sets of emotions at once? Do you have partners for whom this is true? How can you help to ensure that everyone's emotions have space to be processed?

Resist the urge to settle for relationships simply because you don't think you can find better or because you really want to be "actively" polyamorous.

In the past, I settled for relationships with folks because I wanted to "have" something so badly that I would sacrifice my own desires just for the sake of it. I didn't want to be the partner without another partner, my dating options were slim, I desperately wanted to have multiple relationships to prove that I was polyamorous—there were myriad reasons that led to me accepting what was available instead of choosing my own fulfillment. ❉ All relationships are a roll of the dice, but some you can clearly see won't work for you even before they start. Maybe you don't want to be in a hierarchical setup. Maybe you don't want partners who aren't out. Maybe you want a closed dynamic. Maybe you don't want to date monogamous people. Maybe you don't want to date folks who are traditionally married or partnered. Whatever your desire is, hold on to that. Don't allow the desperation to "have" propel you to accept relationships that include things that clearly don't work for you. You don't have to settle.

Have you ever settled for relationships that didn't fulfill your needs? If so, why? How do you avoid settling?

In polyamorous relationships, especially non-nested or long-distance ones, it's not unusual to try to cram the entirety of the relationship into the short periods of time you get to spend with one another, and that can create problems.

If you only see your partner for an evening once a week or one weekend every few weeks, it can be hard to feel like you have enough time to do all the things you want and need to do with them in that time. Catching up, going on a date, resolving any conflicts, sex, helping each other with life things—these all take time, and it can feel like you have to choose a few things to do and let go of others. Often, we choose the fun stuff because we don't want to spend our short time together dealing with the not-fun stuff, but that can mean issues that need addressing don't get dealt with. ❧ It's important to work with our partners on how to have full relationships in the context of the time we have with them. It takes some collaboration and creativity but it's worth it. Learn to be at peace with what happens in the time you spend together and don't become too anxious or fixated on what you did or didn't get to do.

Do you try to cram the entirety of the relationship experience you want with your partners into the limited space of time you may have with them? What drives that desire?

It's important to acknowledge both the intent behind our choices and the impact our choices have. Even if our original intent isn't to cause harm, we can cause harm if we aren't mindful.

Imagine that your partner is upset because you went to see a movie that they really wanted to see with another partner. Notice I didn't say that they were upset at you, just upset. When they express their hurt feelings, instead of acknowledging them, you become distant and harsh, or even tell them their feelings aren't your problem. You didn't mean to hurt them by going to the movies, but the way you responded to their feelings caused them to feel further hurt. ❀ Acknowledging the impact of your actions isn't the same as taking responsibility for it. You don't have to accept blame for the hurt, but you can witness it. That way, your response to the impact is in alignment with your original intent of not causing harm in making the choice. ❀ This can be hard to do if your partner is directly blaming you for their feelings, accusing you of wrong when you weren't wrong or trying to make you be responsible for their feelings. Therefore, it's important to be secure in our intentions, firm in what we know is "ours" and what's "theirs" and solid in being able to hold our own "truths" and our partners' "truths" as equally valid.

Does acknowledging the impact of your choices sometimes feel like assuming responsibility for the feelings of others? How can you separate the two?

Day 74

Having multiple partners is not the sole benefit of practicing nonmonogamy, and the more you grasp this concept, the more you'll enjoy your experience.

Having multiple partners is only one benefit of polyamory and it isn't even the most consistent one in my experience. Some of the most important benefits I've received from polyamory have nothing to do with anyone else and everything to do with myself. Growth, unlearning harmful relationship beliefs and deeper self-awareness are all things I've experienced whether I had one partner or five. ❀ When we hold having multiple partners as the most important benefit of nonmonogamy, we can gloss over the many other things that it can provide. I enjoy my experience of polyamory even more when I remember this.

What are some benefits you receive from polyamory that aren't about having multiple partners?

Being polyamorous doesn't mean you have to martyr yourself for your partners' other relationships. If doing something will cause you too much pain, acknowledge that and say no.

I see this often and even recognize times when I have engaged in martyr behavior. It always had disastrous consequences, both for myself and my partners. It took me some time to learn the difference between challenging myself to grow in polyamory and sacrificing myself on the altar of trying to be a "good" polyamorous person. ❧ It does no one any favors to injure ourselves mentally, emotionally and/or physically rather than accepting where we authentically are. ❧ It's OK to say you're not in a place to meet your partner's new partner. It's OK to say no to group sexual encounters you don't wish to be a part of. It's OK to say no to someone you don't want to live with moving into your house. It's OK to say you don't want your spouse going on the vacation that you had planned together with someone else. Learn to embrace your authentic no.

Do you martyr yourself for your other relationships? If so, what do you get from doing that?

Day 76

It is not our partners' job to uphold our boundaries. It is our job to define and maintain our boundaries and our partners' job to honor and respect them.

Say you have a yard and you put up a fence around it. Your neighbors are expected to respect that fence and not cross it unless invited. They are expected not to damage the fence, nor push you to move it. But the maintenance of the fence is all your responsibility. You can't expect your neighbors to do the labor of painting or repairing your fence. They have their own fences to maintain. It's the same with our boundaries. Once we indicate that we have a boundary, it is our job to uphold it. ❧ Many times, people will erect a boundary, but they won't uphold it or reinforce it. Then when someone crosses it, they'll be upset with that person. The true issue is that they didn't hold the boundary strongly. If you aren't clear and firm with your boundaries, how can you expect someone to honor them? ❧ Note that this doesn't excuse abusive behavior. Just because someone has poor boundary-setting abilities, that doesn't give you the right to run all over them. If someone can't set firm boundaries for themselves, as a decent person there are some things that you just shouldn't do to anyone, whether they allow it or not.

What does boundary maintenance look like for you?

Sometimes, it's not the thing our partner did that made us uncomfortable, it's the fact that they did it with someone else rather than us that's bothering us.

It's important to understand that our partners are people on their own journeys. They get to decide what experiences they want to have, as well as when, how and with whom. Sometimes, our partners will choose to do things with others. Instead of feeling slighted that we weren't the person they chose for an activity, focus on your partner having experiences that enrich them and having people they can share those experiences with. You also will continue to have new experiences with them. ❧ Plus, if it's something you also wish to do with them, now you know that they are open to it (although they also have the right to choose to do different things with different people). If you do it together, it will still be unique because you are what makes the experience of it together different.

When your partners do new things with others, do you find yourself feeling uncomfortable? If so, why?

You partners may meet people who they find more attractive than you in some way, who they have better sex with or who they have more things in common with. None of these mean that they now see you as "less."

Truth is, there is always going to be someone out there who is more attractive than you, "better" in bed than you or more suited for your partner in some way, and your partners may even feel that way about another partner. But that doesn't mean that you are of lesser value to them. ❦ The goal isn't to compete with the people our partners interact with and make sure that we are always the "most" of anything to them, but to be in collaboration with their other folks to contribute to their joy. What matters is that our partners continue to indicate that they value us and what we have with them. ❦ I also find that we are usually the ones comparing ourselves and finding ways that we are "less than" our partners' other folks, and that our partners don't see it that way at all. They just see their various partners as different. ❦ Asking, "Is so-and-so prettier/better in bed/more enjoyable than me?" has never helped me to feel better about myself. Ask yourself why you feel you need to know this. How do you think your partner feels when you ask them questions like this? How would you feel if your partner asked you this?

Do you struggle with feeling "less than" when making comparisons to the other people your partners interact with? Why do you feel the need to "measure up"?

Sometimes in relationships, we can become so skilled at navigating and avoiding conflict that we fail to take a critical look at why conflict is happening to begin with.

When my marriage ended, it was strange. We didn't fight often. We had learned better ways to communicate. I had done a lot of work to manage my emotions in ways that were healthy and constructive. It almost didn't make sense to me. It took some time to reflect and realize that we had become skilled at navigating conflict and at taking steps to avoid it, but when it did happen, it always stemmed from the reality that we had deeply fundamental incompatibilities and no amount of conflict strategy was going to fix that. ❧ Conflict, while uncomfortable, is unavoidable and necessary. It can illuminate things that we weren't aware of and it can show us things we need to see but maybe have been trying not to see. While it is important to learn how to navigate conflict and how to avoid it, we also must learn to listen to it. It happens for a reason and being unwilling to look at those reasons can be a trap that leads to more conflict and heartache down the line. ❧ Be brave enough to look at what is going on when you are in conflict with someone. And then be brave enough to face what you see.

Do you view conflict as a necessary and revelatory part of your relationships? What causes you to want to avoid conflict?

Our partners can sometimes be confused or surprised by how upset we are about an issue, especially if they didn't know how important or sensitive it was to us. That doesn't mean they are trying to be dismissive or uncaring.

In a former relationship, my partner become very upset about me going to an event and meeting someone whom I began dating. It turns out that my partner had always wanted to go to that event and never had anyone to go with, something I didn't know. I was so surprised by how bothered he was that my initial response was one of shock and not empathy. ❧ When we are strongly activated by something our partners have done, it can sometimes be a surprise to us how bothered we are. In these situations, it will definitely be a surprise to our partner, especially if it's a new sensitivity we have just become aware of by the incident or is something we weren't aware we valued so highly until that moment. When this happens, our partners are likely to be confused about our feelings and struggle to respond to them. Understanding this is helpful for everyone. ❧ It's also OK to say, "I'm surprised by how upset this made you, but that in no way means I don't think your feelings about it are valid."

Have you ever been surprised by how upset a partner was about something you thought wasn't a big deal? How did you respond?

If you make changes that drastically alter the nature of your relationship with a person, they have a right to respond to those changes in a way that enables them to accept your terms while honoring their needs.

Discovering that you want to be polyamorous while in a monogamous relationship. Realizing you want to live with multiple partners when you're in a nested relationship with someone who doesn't want that. Deciding that you no longer want relationships that prescribe a hierarchy when you are in a relationship that was previously "primary." These are all valid choices, and you are free to make them. ❧ What you are *not* free to do is decide how your partner should respond to these changes or declare that they are wrong for making their own changes to protect themselves and their relationship desires. We are free to make our own choices, but we also have to acknowledge that those choices will have consequences. You don't owe your partners relationships that you don't want to engage in, but they don't owe you that either. Relationships aren't a la carte menus where we can add and remove things at will without our partners having their own responses to those additions or subtractions. ❧ Folks get to decide that they don't want what you are now offering to them if it's not in alignment with what they also want. ❧ Note that if your partner responds to your changes by subjecting you to abuse, that is absolutely not OK.

Do changes in your relationship cause fear or anxiety for you? How do you face that fear?

Resist the urge to try to keep your relationships "perfect" because you fear your partners will enjoy their other relationships more than the relationship they have with you if conflict occurs.

Most people try to avoid conflict in their relationships, but I find that this is especially true in polyamorous relationships. Often, there is a heightened fear of conflict with our partners because we don't want to be the "problem child" partner while their other relationships are going smoothly. ❧ It's important to remember that all relationships have ebbs and flows, highs and lows, and that sometimes conflict is unavoidable and necessary for growth. Just because you and a partner are experiencing difficulty, it doesn't mean that they now love or enjoy you less and someone else more. All relationships will experience conflict at some point. That would be true even if you had no additional partners except each other. And your partners will also go through times of difficulty in their other relationships. ❧ Trying to maintain a perfect relationship with someone is exhausting, creates a false facade and doesn't honor your genuine needs. If you believe that your relationship with someone isn't strong enough to handle times of conflict, or that your partners aren't able to love you and others while you are going through conflict, maybe that isn't a relationship you need to be in.

Do you try to keep your relationships "perfect"?
How does that impact your experience of them?

It's impossible to feel secure in a relationship with someone whom you believe is worth more than you are.

If you believe the person you're with is more valuable than you, you will always struggle to believe in what they see in you. You might worry that someone else of more value than you will come along and your partner will choose them over you, and you may fear that your partner will realize you are "beneath" them and leave. Until you are fully acquainted with your worth and stop seeing others as more valuable than you, you will constantly struggle to feel secure in relationships. ❧ Believe that your partners have chosen you because they deem you worthy of them. If you don't, ask yourself why you want to be in a relationship with someone who thinks you are of less value than they are. Work on your self-worth so you can choose relationships that reflect your value of yourself. ❧ I also want to acknowledge that if you have a marginalized identity or multiple marginalized identities, believing in your own self-worth is going to be that much harder because you live in a world that is constantly reinforcing that you are of little to no value.

Do your relationships reflect your belief in your own worth?
Do you see your partners as of higher value than you?
How can you improve your estimation of yourself?

Compersion isn't necessary to navigate polyamory successfully, does not need to be cultivated if you don't feel the need to do so and can be felt simultaneously alongside jealousy.

When I first began my polyamorous journey, I would see all these people posting about compersion. I tried to fake it until I felt it. That never worked and usually resulted in uncomfortable situations because I was lying to my partners and myself about what I was authentically feeling. I finally realized that I just don't experience compersion much and that it wasn't necessary for me to do so to have a peaceful and happy polyamorous existence. ❀ I experience compersion now, but it wasn't something I cultivated. It just happened. I have also observed that it's not the opposite of jealousy—I can feel compersive and jealous at the same time. And my ability to feel compersion is influenced by a variety of things, like if I'm feeling secure and fulfilled in my relationship with my partner, how I feel about my metamour, what is going on in my individual polyamorous journey and more. ❀ I'm happy that my partners are making decisions that make them happy. I want them to have relationships that are good for them and I am OK if that sometimes makes me feel uncomfortable. What's important is that I support their autonomy and maintain my autonomy to feel how I genuinely feel about it.

What is your relationship with compersion like?

**I am ultimately responsible for making myself happy.
Part of that responsibility to myself is ensuring that I am
in relationships with people who overall bring me joy.**

This goes for any relationship, romantic or platonic. No one
is supposed to make us happy and our happiness is ours
to manage. But if you are in a bunch of relationships with
folks who don't contribute to your overall joy, happiness
will be hard to come by. We need a balance of having
happiness within and happiness outside of ourselves. ✻
When I am no longer able to say that a partner contributes
to my joy, it is up to me to decide what to do about that.
Maybe I need to end that relationship, maybe I need to
adjust what I expect from that person so I am happy with
what they are bringing to me in the present moment,
maybe I need to work with them to see if it's possible to
bring that relationship back to a place of overall joy (if
they also want to do that work). In all instances, the onus
of responsibility is still on me, but I accept and address
that for my happiness to continue, something about the
relationship needs to change.

How do you hold yourself accountable to ensuring
that you are responsible for your happiness?

We are not responsible for the feelings of our partners, but our actions contribute to and affect their emotional state. Acknowledging this is expressing care.

I do not feel a sense of responsibility for the feelings of my partners, but I do feel a sense of responsibility *to* the feelings of my partners. What that means is that I am going to own when something I did had an impact on their emotions, I am going to exhibit care for their feelings when they share them with me, I am going to offer support where I can and I am going to endeavor to not be defensive or dismissive when they share their feelings with me. ❀ If we claim to care about a person, that means we care about all of them, feelings too. Not being responsible for another's emotions doesn't mean being careless or inconsiderate of them. Be mindful of the distinction.

Do you struggle with differentiating between being responsible for your partner's emotions and being mindful of them? What is the distinction to you?

It is OK to ask your partners for focused time with you and to ask to have your time with them be respected.

Barring an emergency, it is reasonable to ask that your quality time with a person be focused if that's important to you. It can be hard to feel like you're spending time with someone if they are communicating with someone else while you're together. It is also reasonable to ask that your time be respected by your partner. ❧ Arbitrarily changing dates, ending dates earlier than agreed upon or canceling dates due to the emotions of another person are not things you just have to put up with, especially as a "secondary" partner, single or solo-poly person, or non-nested partner. It is frustrating to have your dates interrupted by calls that could have waited, discover that a meta will be joining you when you weren't consulted or hear your partner's phone going off repeatedly while you're trying to enjoy your time with them. ❧ Nested and "primary" partners can also experience a lack of commitment to their time with their partner. Sometimes, we can bring more intentionality and focus to our time with our non-nested or "secondary" partners than we do to our nested ones. We take for granted that because they are always around, we can be more cavalier with our time with them.

What are ways that make you feel like your partner is focusing on you when you are together?

Day 88

Your partner experiencing less jealousy than you do doesn't mean that they care less about you than you do about them. Jealousy (or lack of) means different things for different people.

I have always struggled more with jealousy than my partners. It used to really bother me that they almost never experienced it or experienced it in a milder way than I did. It was hard for some of my partners to empathize with my jealousy and it also made me feel like they cared less about me than I did about them. ❀ I used to believe (and to some extent still do) that lack of jealousy meant that the person didn't care as much about me because the thought of losing me or having our relationship "threatened" wasn't scary to them. ❀ I have come to realize that some people have more secure relationship attachments, feel jealousy to a very small degree or not at all, have a negative connotation to jealousy and so they work really hard not to feel it, or just see things differently than I do. Everyone has an emotional index. Some people feel a lot of jealousy and some people feel little to no jealousy at all. Neither way is bad or good, wrong or right. We're just human beings being different human beings. Jealousy is just an emotion, same as any other. It's what we do with it that counts.

What does jealousy mean to you? When do you experience it?

Resist the urge to withdraw from your partners when they return from being with others. Instead, draw near to them to be reminded that they still desire to be close to you even as they are close to others.

Imagine that you're on the playground with a friend and you're playing ball together. The friend sees another friend and they run off to play with them for a while. Afterward, they come back to play with you again, but you're upset because they were playing with someone else. Instead of returning to joyfully playing together, you pout, take your ball and stalk off to the edge of the playground sulking, even though you really want to play with your friend again. ❧ When my partners are off enjoying their relationships with others, it can sometimes put me in my "baby" feelings, thinking that they care for those people more than me. This can cause me to withdraw from them in protest. But deep down, what I really need is to get close to my partners to be reminded that we still have a connection too. When I bypass that initial urge and draw near to them, it helps me to remember our connection and feel more secure. ❧ This wasn't an easy path for me. I had to learn not to reach out before I was ready to really reconnect because that had some bad outcomes. But when I kept this concept in my mind and worked on it little by little, I found it incredibly useful.

Do you withdraw from your partners when they return from being with others? How can you reestablish your connection?

Polyamory works best when we consider why we need something from our partners in response to their being with others, even if at the end of that inquiry, we determine that what we're asking for is still necessary.

Someone asked the members in an online polyamory group if it was OK to request a 24-hour period of space from interacting with their partner after that partner had been intimate with someone else. This is a common question from folks new to polyamory. While technically, there isn't anything wrong with asking for this, it serves us better to ask ourselves why we need this space and understand where the desire to create distance is coming from. ❧ Oftentimes, there's a deeper need underneath the surface that we should be addressing. When we seek ways to be "OK" with what our partners have going on with others, we're often struggling with things like needing assurance that they still love us, desiring space to acknowledge that we're struggling or feeling threatened that our partner will leave us for another. ❧ Sometimes, when we dig a little deeper, we discover that what we need isn't what we were asking for. And sometimes, we discover that what we thought we needed doesn't change at all, but at least we know where the need stems from.

What are the deeper needs behind some of the requests you have made of your partners to accommodate you?

Day 91

It's OK if you want to ask your partners to adjust their interactions with others for the sake of your emotional, physical or mental wellness. Your partners get to say "no," but you still get to ask.

"My mental health has been particularly affected recently. Can you hold off on forming new connections while I'm working on getting it managed again?" ❀ "I'm immuno-compromised and we're in a pandemic. Can you pause meeting new people in person?" ❀ Sometimes we feel the need to make requests of our partners to adjust their relationships with others for our sake. While I believe some requests are unreasonable, unrealistic or unacceptable, people still get to ask for what they believe they need. Notice that I said "ask" and not "demand." ❀ Our partners get to decide what they are genuinely willing to do to support us, especially as it relates to others whose needs they also care about. And our partners saying "no" to our requests doesn't automatically mean they don't care about us. ❀ It's also OK if you find these requests completely unreasonable for you no matter what they are. If that's the case, choose to be in relationships with folks who also see making these requests as unreasonable.

Do you think it's reasonable or unreasonable for partners to make requests like these? Why or why not?

When we are in conflict with our partners, our sense of connection with them is ruptured. In these moments it can be helpful to set an intention of returning to connection with each other.

When in conflict with my partners, I set the intention of connection. I remind myself and them that we are addressing this issue and we are working through it because we are trying to establish, reestablish, maintain and honor our connection to each other. ❀ It can be easy to forget that we are connected to each other in those moments because we are struggling to *feel* connected to them, which is likely why we are in conflict to begin with. Setting the intention of connection impacts everything from the language we use to the compassion, grace and empathy we hold for them and for ourselves, to the way we come together after the conflict has been resolved. It is remembering that this person is someone we care about and who cares about us. ❀ I also want to add that we should extend the intention of connection to ourselves. If we are in a relationship in which maintaining a connection means being disconnected from ourselves, that is not true connection. It's important to set the intention of being in relationships with others that also allow us to be connected to ourselves.

Do you struggle to remember connection in conflict with your partners? How do you feel connected to them even in conflict?

Let love grow. Let love connect. Let love expand. Let love be boundless. When it is allowed to have wings and soar, love is beautiful to behold.

One of my partners went to visit their other partner in California and they got the opportunity to meet one of *my* partners, who also lives there, for the first time. My partners and my metamours spent a day getting to know one another. I was so excited for them to meet because I knew they all would really enjoy each other's company. My metamour sent me a picture of the four of them together, smiling at the camera. I saw all these people I love connecting with one another and I wasn't there. While I would have loved to have been there and I missed them all so much, my heart was fit to bursting with joy at seeing them. I thought I would feel sad or envious or left out, but I just felt an overwhelming sense of elation. ❋ In a way, I was there. The love I have for all of them was with each of them. It made me grateful for the life I live, where love is allowed the room to breathe, to blossom, to extend, to multiply.

How do you cultivate the love in your life being free to soar?

Sometimes, you can find yourself in relationships where the fear of losing the other person causes you to lose yourself. That is too high a price to pay, and true love doesn't require that.

I believe that a lot of the indignation folks experience when relationships end comes from the acknowledgment that they gave up so much of themselves in the relationship through fear of losing their partner and still, they lost them anyway. It feels like an injustice. ❋ This is why maintaining a firm hold on who you are is so crucial in forming relationships with others—particularly in the case of nonmonogamy, where there are more people to be afraid to lose and more opportunities to lose yourself in trying to keep them. The only way you can know if someone can truly hold you is if you truly hold yourself. ❋ Don't lose yourself for someone else. Be in relationships where you can love yourself and others at the same time.

Do you give up parts of yourself in your relationships because you are afraid to lose your loved ones? If so, how does that impact your relationship with yourself?

You can't love someone into falling out of love with someone else.

There are many ways that this can happen: Monogamous people engaging in relationships with polyamorous people and thinking they can love them away from their current partners back to monogamy, new partners thinking they can love a person into getting over an ex, someone thinking that they can love their partner away from someone their partner is in a harmful relationship with. Somehow, we believe we can love people out of love with the other people they hold in their heart. ❀ But love doesn't work like that, and neither do our hearts. How many have struggled with wishing they could figure out how to not love someone? Imagine, then, how much more unlikely it is that you can somehow do this *for* someone. ❀ Loving a heart means accepting the state it's in and the people it contains. We may be uncomfortable about that, but claiming to care for a person while trying to change them isn't embracing who they really are. Honestly, we want to do this is because we're afraid there isn't room in their heart for us, so we try to take over. ❀ Let your partners' hearts hold what they hold. If there's genuine room for you, you won't have to gain it by boxing others out.

Have you ever attempted to love someone out of love with someone else? Has anyone ever attempted to love you out of love with someone else? Did it work?

Day 96

Something we have to come to terms with as we establish and maintain healthy boundaries is that we may need to keep people who we really want to be in our life out of it.

Boundaries are always about the question of who is more important—them or me? Is my safety able to be as important as their presence? Am I willing to cede some of my space for this person and I to share space? Is it healthy and mutually fulfilling for us to do so? ❀ When we strengthen our boundary work, it is not uncommon for us to find that some of the people we are currently in relationships with no longer meet the criteria for having a continued presence in our lives or to realize that the relationship we have with them needs to change drastically. ❀ It is sad when we have to lose someone we desire to have in our lives because they can't exist safely within our borders, but it is even sadder when we lose ourselves for someone else. ❀ Perhaps you have a boundary around how folks manage their jealousy with you, how folks communicate with you when they are upset, how transparent a person is with you about their other relationships or how much someone shares about you with other partners. Hold firmly to whatever boundary you have. The right people for you will support you.

How do you uphold your boundaries when you become aware that a person you care about isn't capable of honoring them?

Developing communication skills in polyamory isn't only about learning how to express our needs, wants, boundaries, emotions and vulnerabilities well but also about developing the skill to openly express our desire, appreciation and enthusiasm about our partners, and this can be difficult for some people.

Expressing how much you love someone and how much you desire them can feel as vulnerable as telling someone about a pain you might be feeling. It's important that we challenge ourselves to openly and clearly communicate our regard for our partners, not just assume that they know we care about them because we're in a relationship with them. ❀ When we are in a relationship, we have a "tether" to another person—the line of connection we feel between ourselves and them. In a strong connection, that tether is taut. You can feel the connection to the other person even when they make small movements. As time and life happens, the tethers that connect us to others can become slack. It's important that we tug on those tethers every so often to let the people we are in relationships with know we're still here and that we want to be here. We're saying, "I still want to feel you. Do you feel me?" ❀ People forget, get insecure, life gets in the way, and the tethers slacken. Communicating that you are still feeling your partners goes a long way to help them be more at ease with you being in relationships with others.

How do you struggle to communicate your desire and regard for your partners?

You can recognize that someone is doing their absolute best to be in a relationship with you and also recognize that it isn't enough to meet your needs. Effort is important, but the results of that effort are equally as important.

We can identify that someone is giving us their most valiant effort but also know that it still falls short of what we truly need and value. If you know that you've done your best to communicate your needs clearly and given someone enough time and flexibility to see if they can meet those needs but they just don't seem to be able to, it's OK to acknowledge their effort and still accept that it isn't working for you. ❧ Maybe a person is in several relationships and no matter how hard they try, they aren't able to be available to you the way you need them to be. Maybe you can see that they are working on their jealousy and you don't judge them for how they feel, but it is more than you are willing to navigate. Maybe you need more empathy for your own difficult emotions and try though they might, your partner just can't seem to relate. It's OK to say, "I acknowledge that you are giving me the best that you can, and I thank you for that, but I just need more."

Is the effort made or the results of that effort more important to you? Why?

Day 99

If you are not honest about your genuine desires with your partners because you are afraid they will become upset or disappointed or leave you, you're trading a momentary discomfort for a much larger pain down the road.

Imagine that your partner asks you to agree that you will only go on vacation with each other and not other partners. You don't want to make this agreement, but you also don't want to upset your partner, so you say yes. A few months later, around your birthday, a newer partner has a business commitment in a place you've always wanted to visit and asks if you'd like to tag along as a birthday present. You really want to go, but you have this agreement with your other partner. ❧ If you had been honest with your partner about your lack of desire to make the agreement when it was presented to you, they likely would have gotten upset but they would have either figured out how to move forward, or in the event they did decide to end their relationship with you, you would have had room to create partnerships that support your genuine desires. ❧ Now, not only do you have to end the agreement and likely disappoint them, but you also have to deal with them possibly feeling lied to because of your dishonesty in the first place. Be honest about what you really want, even when it's the more difficult conversation.

Do you sometimes trade honesty for temporary comfort with your partners? What about being honest scares you?

When I'm struggling to reconnect with a partner after they've been with someone else, I ask myself, "Do I want to be in my feelings about what they're doing with someone else, or do I just want to enjoy my time with them?"

Early in my journey, I often found that I would struggle to reconnect with my partners when they had been with others. An acquaintance shared some wisdom with me about this. They told me that when this would happen to them, they had to learn to bypass their initial impulse to withdraw and instead reach out for connection with their partner because that was what they needed. ❧ Just asking myself whether I want to be in my feelings or to enjoy time with my partner helps me identify what is important to me at that moment. Sometimes the answer is to be in my feelings. When that is the case, I honor that need and either request space from my partner while I process my emotions or seek their support. ❧ Often, however, I find that my answer is that I want to enjoy my time with my partner. I release my hold on my discomfort and proceed with the interaction that matters most to me—reconnecting with my loved one and reminding myself that they can be in their connection with others and still be in connection with me.

Do you struggle to reconnect with partners after they've been with others? How do you enjoy reconnecting with partners after they've been with others?

The true blessing of being honest about our feelings or asking for what we need comes from having the courage to be vulnerable, advocating for ourselves and honoring who we are.

My communication with a person is about me. Expressing my feelings or asking for what I need is about being authentic to myself and less about the response from others. I'm not saying that being understood or having your requests granted isn't important, but it is equally important (and sometimes more so) to value what the purpose of communicating these things is for *you*, even if the other person doesn't respond how you wish them to. ❧ So often people will say, "I asked for what I needed and they didn't give it to me. Asking is useless," or "How can I ask for this in a way that will guarantee they give it to me?" To me, it's not about the outcome. It's about me advocating for myself. If that is all that occurred, I see that as a personal success. ❧ People will share their feelings and if they find themselves misunderstood, they can see the sharing of the feelings as the problem. To me, the success of sharing my feelings comes from me having the courage to do so. When I make it about me standing up for myself, it's always worthwhile.

What is the merit of communication for you?
What value does it have for you personally?

Conversations around conflict in nonmonogamy can be navigated much more smoothly when we view them as invitations to our partners to understand us and for us to understand them.

When we are in conflict with our partners or need to communicate with them about difficult emotions, one of the most primary needs we have is to be understood. We can view these situations as an invitation for understanding, both of ourselves and our partners. ❧ When you extend an invitation to someone, it's because you want them to attend an event. As such, the invitation is designed to appeal to the invitee and entice them to come to the occasion. ❧ Consider how we can communicate in a way that makes our "invitation" appealing to our partners, so that they want to attend the understanding of us and the sharing of themselves. ❧ When we use language that is hostile, accusatory, unkind, dismissive or invalidating, we ensure that our invitation to understanding will be met with a refusal. We activate defensiveness instead of vulnerability and openness. If you want to be seen and also see others, make sure that your desire is expressed in a way that is inviting and fosters coming together and closeness, not retreat and separation.

When communicating with your partners, how can you speak to them to invite understanding?

Even with the best of intentions, it is not possible for our partners to be available or capable of processing our every emotion around nonmonogamy with us. Having a polyamory support network is vital.

By far, the relationships that have been the most fulfilling and consistent since I have become nonmonogamous have been the friendships I have made in the polyamorous community. My friends have been sources of support, wisdom, validation and perspective. They provide safe places to vent when I need to. ❀ So much of the focus in nonmonogamy is on how to establish multiple partnerships, but developing polyamorous friendships is crucial. One of the first tips I tell folks new to polyamory is to find other polyamorous folks to be friends with. Our partners can't be our only source of support in nonmonogamy, even if they may wish to be. Partners may be incapable of or unwilling to process our emotions to the extent that we want them to, and they have the right to boundaries around how much processing they can do with us. ❀ It's invaluable to have someone besides your partners to call when you're struggling, or someone who will offer you perspective or reassurance when you are feeling threatened or insecure. Whether it's friends, a coach or peer-support person, or a polyamory-friendly therapist, build a support network you can rely on so you have a group of caring people available to help.

Who is in your polyamorous support network?

You are not responsible for managing your partners' guilt in nonmonogamy, especially if that means silencing or not honoring your genuine emotions.

The topic of guilt comes up often in nonmonogamy. Many people feel guilty for being in nonmonogamous relationships even as they know they are doing nothing wrong. ❧ Similarly, we can sometimes hide or not be fully honest about our feelings with our partners because we don't want to make them feel guilty or like they are doing something wrong. But that causes us to not honor our own feelings for the sake of managing someone else's. ❧ If you did your best to communicate your feelings in a constructive way and acknowledge your partners' autonomy, then whatever guilt they may be feeling is theirs to work through. If you know you weren't trying to make them feel bad but just trying to be honest and vulnerable with them without accusation of wrongdoing, then they need to examine why they feel guilty about doing something they were free to do, even if it made you uncomfortable. ❧ The work of nonmonogamy includes us learning how to own our choices for ourselves and our happiness, even as we know those choices may sometimes result in the discomfort or displeasure of our partners. We're all responsible for developing the skill of being able to care about our partners' emotions without feeling responsible for them or guilty about them.

How do you respond if a partner feels guilty that you are uncomfortable with something that they are doing?

You don't always need to "get something" from your partner's nonmonogamy in order to appreciate, validate and support it.

A common question from monogamous folks to non-monogamous people is, "What do you get from letting your partner be with others?" ❧ Early on in my journey, this was a question I would ask myself often, especially during times when my partner had a partner and I didn't or when they had a date while I was at home. "What do I get out of them being with someone else?" It was like I needed a tangible benefit to make dealing with it seem worth it. ❧ You can answer the question by saying you get to have your freedom with others too, or that you get a partner who's happier, or whatever benefit you perceive. But consider why we have to get something from our partner's nonmonogamy at all. Our partners do many things to enrich their lives that we don't get any tangible benefit from. We don't necessarily get anything from them going out with their friends. We don't get anything from them reading a book or going on a hike. So why do we feel the necessity to get something from their relationships with others to make "allowing" their freedom in nonmonogamy worthwhile? ❧ Not everything is about us. Our partners aren't supposed to exist solely for our benefit.

Do you feel like you need to get something from your partners' nonmonogamy in order to make it worthwhile for you? What should you get?

If you've asked your partners for a specific action to help you feel reassured and cared for as they relate to others, make sure you are responding with gratitude and encouragement when they give it to you. Positive reinforcement goes a long way.

You tell your nesting partner that when they come home from a date, it would help you feel reassured if they gave you a hug and told you that they missed you. The next time they come home from their other partner's place, that's what they do. Instead of you responding with gratitude, however, you say, "You're only doing this because I asked you to do it." Sound familiar? ❋ If we ask our partners for a consideration and they lovingly give that to us, it is hurtful to then slap it away. Asking someone to give you a thing only to reject it when offered is confusing and can be damaging to them. It makes the other person unsure of how to care for you and can result in them not trusting what you say and being less inclined to care for your needs when you ask for things. If you're just going to reject it anyway, why bother? ❋ I understand that it can be hard to identify what we need in nonmonogamy. Sometimes, we ask for a particular thing and then when we get it, it doesn't land the way we thought it would. Still, receive the care offered with gratitude and then acknowledge that you may need something different than you initially thought.

How can you positively reinforce your partners when they show up in ways that you have asked for?

Day 107

It is OK to take time to reorganize your feelings for a person after a breakup or relationship transition and to ask for minimum to no contact with them while you do so.

When my husband broke up with me, I immediately shifted to this frenzied space of "We have to figure out how to be friends now!" I was pushy about it and I ended up driving him further away. Frankly, it was too soon for either of us to consider what we wanted our new relationship to look like. We hadn't even processed the end of the old one. ☀ It's OK to need time to restructure your feelings for a person after a relationship ends or transitions and to ask for little to no contact during that time. In polyamory, there's a lot of emphasis on remaining friends with exes, and people often don't account for the fact that this is usually a process that happens over time, sometimes with periods of not interacting with one another. The nonmonogamy community can feel small at times, which can make it hard to get that space from an ex. ☀ You aren't immature if you need space to get over a person. Do what is necessary to care for your own heart. A person who genuinely cares for you will understand and honor your request. And once you have tended to your heart, you can revisit what a new path forward looks like for you both from a more healed, centered space.

What are your needs for space after breaking up with someone?

How your partners show up to you is not always a reflection of what you're worth or what you deserve. A person's behavior is usually a reflection of who they are, not who you are.

A dear friend once told me, "How a person is showing up to me is not always in direct correlation to what I deserve." I have kept this in mind when I find myself struggling with the way a person is treating me. I often find that when someone I'm dating or interacting with isn't treating me how I want them to, I internalize it as there being something wrong with me. If there wasn't, they'd be giving me what I wanted from them, right? ❧ Now, I understand that someone else's behavior doesn't determine what I deserve. And I know that someone else's behavior isn't a reflection of who I am, but who they are. With that understanding, I am more at peace about the choices of others and I also honor myself more fully because I'm not letting the choices of others determine what I believe I am worth. I determine that for myself and then respond accordingly when someone isn't meeting that standard and have gratitude when someone is. ❧ People can sometimes use this sentiment to justify their own poor treatment of others and gaslight folks when they have reasonable reactions to being harmed by them. If you're treating someone poorly and they are responding to that, that's definitely a you thing.

Do you internalize how others treat you as what you deserve from them? If so, does positive treatment hold as much weight as negative treatment?

The most important person I need to understand why I'm nonmonogamous is myself. I can't make a person understand my nonmonogamy and I honestly don't need them to.

Something I find perplexing is how much time nonmonogamous people spend talking about monogamy. Pondering on it, explaining it, breaking it down, sharing opinions on it. I find this to be peculiar because, outside of needing to understand the ways in which monogamous conditioning influences how I show up to my nonmonogamous relationships and working through unpacking that and assessing the impact it has on my relationships, I don't spend a lot of time thinking about a relationship orientation that I have no interest in. ❧ I also don't feel the need to justify, explain or try to get people to understand why I'm non-monogamous. I'm nonmonogamous because that's what works for me. I may attempt to go into more detail with a person about why I'm nonmonogamous, but I don't believe it is my responsibility to make them get it. Some will, some won't. I don't need another person's understanding of it to validate that it is right for me. ❧ The most important person I want to have a true understanding of why I'm nonmonogamous is myself. My own understanding of my nonmonogamous identity is what truly matters to me. When I am rooted in that understanding of myself, I find it's easier to align with folks who get me and also to accept when folks don't.

Do you feel a sense of pressure to explain, represent or defend nonmonogamy? Why?

If someone wants "more" of a relationship with you than you want with them, it's OK to say no. If someone wants "less" of a relationship with you than you want with them, it's also OK to say no.

We don't owe anyone any kind of relationship other than the one we authentically and enthusiastically wish to participate in with them. Sometimes people want "more" or "less" of a relationship with us than we want with them and it's OK to say, "No, I don't wish to have that with you," or "No, I am unable to accept what you're offering." ❧ Maybe a person wants more time than you are willing to spend with them, or they want to be a committed partner but you want a casual relationship with them. Perhaps they want more intimacy with you but you aren't there yet or don't want that level of intimacy with them. Honor your desires and be upfront about them. ❧ This is also true in the reverse. Maybe someone wants to remain casual with you but you have more than casual feelings for them. Or they want you to have a "comet" relationship but you want a more integrated partnership. Perhaps they just want to be friends and you have more romantic feelings for them and can't accept that. Honor your desires and be upfront about them.

Do you honor your genuine relationship desires when connecting with others or do you place their wishes above yours? How can you balance making both equally important?

In nonmonogamy, a partner who has other partners breaking up with us can cause acute feelings of rejection because they are choosing others in a way that they no longer wish to be with us.

One day, I was scrolling through my Instagram timeline and saw a photo of my husband (whom I'm separating from) and my former metamour smiling in a selfie on a hike. On the one hand, I was genuinely happy for them. But on the other hand, it was hard for me to see. It felt unfair in a way. ❧ My husband's choice to end things with me while still maintaining his romantic relationships with others made the rejection I felt especially sharp. It's not like he didn't want a romantic relationship of any kind, he just didn't want one with me. Accepting that has been a challenge. ❧ I remind myself that we all have a timeline in our relationships and that he and I reached the end of ours. Others will have their own timelines with him. I also remember that I ultimately want to be with people who authentically and enthusiastically choose me. When someone is no longer able to do that, it's better for both of us to acknowledge it and move on.

Do breakups feel more or less acute for you in nonmonogamy? Why?

Being the partner without another partner can be hard in nonmonogamy. It's OK and possible to be supportive of your partners' relationships with others but disappointed in your own lack of "success" in finding relationships.

I've been here quite a few times along my journey. It can be an uncomfortable space to sit in. It's easier for me now than it was in the beginning, but it still has its challenges. ❧ Remember that every nonmonogamy journey is individual and yours will develop in its own time. Be honest about your feelings. Understand that you can feel supportive of your partners' "success" and disappointed about your lack of it at the same time and both feelings are valid. Manage your boundaries around exposure to your partners' other relationships and only interact with them as much as you can without it negatively affecting your emotional state. ❧ Also, remember that nonmonogamy is about more than having multiple partners. It's also about learning how to support our partners in their relationships and about reconciling our own beliefs about relationships, whether we are in five relationships or none. And try to keep hope alive. Believe that your time will come and think of how you would want your partner to support you if the roles were reversed.

Have you ever been the "partner without another partner"? Was it challenging for you? Why or why not?

It is possible for a person to operate in relationships in ways that aren't objectively wrong, but that are wrong for you.

I once told a story about when my husband didn't communicate with me before changing his life insurance policy to add one of his partners as a beneficiary. I shared my experience of struggling with that and eventually coming to accept it. Several people opined that he was wrong for not talking to me about it first. I don't agree. While it did bother me that he didn't talk to me about it first, I don't believe he was wrong for choosing not to talk to me about it before making his decision. What was wrong for me, however, was the fact that he didn't talk to me before he did it. I would have liked him to tell me before changing the policy, not later. Our communication beliefs were incompatible. ❀ There's a difference between someone behaving in a way that's wrong and them behaving in a way that's wrong for you. One view creates a villain/victim dichotomy. The other view comprehends that humans are different and some things work for us and some don't, but that doesn't mean folks (or ourselves) are bad people. ❀ This isn't to say that anything can be acceptable and that there are no relationship behaviors that are outright wrong. Manipulation, gaslighting, breaking agreements and violating boundaries are not OK.

Are you able to discern when someone is behaving toward you in a way that isn't "wrong" but is wrong for you? How do you navigate that?

When we are upset about an issue in our relationships, we can sometimes erroneously direct our frustrations at our metamours when really, the issue is with our partners.

Often, we can get upset with our metamours for issues that are really with our partners. It's easier to direct your ire at another person indirectly than to be upset at the person you directly love and care about. We can avoid recognizing that someone we love is doing something that causes us pain. ❀ When you find yourself upset with a metamour, examine if your issue is actually with them or with your partner and the way they are treating you. While I genuinely believe that part of being a caring metamour is showing concern that your partners are treating their other partners well—and I wouldn't personally keep a partner who I thought treated their other partners poorly—I understand that it isn't anyone else's job to make sure I am being treated well by someone. That responsibility lies between me and my partners.

Have you ever had a metamour be angry with you when the real issue was the actions of your shared partner? What was the situation and how was it resolved?

Our desire and capacity for romance, sex, intimacy, connection and vulnerability is highly individual and will shift as we move through life. The same is true for our partners. Don't judge them based on you, and don't judge yourself based on them.

This plays out in so many ways. We project our desires and capacity onto our partners and don't understand why they operate differently from the way we do. Sometimes, we even judge and condemn them for being different than we are in this way. ❧ Maybe you have a partner largely interested in casual sexual relationships and you wish they would have more steady partnerships. Maybe you have a partner who desires deeply loving and emotional relationships and you wish they just wanted casual ones. Maybe you're a nonmonogamous person with a monogamous partner and you wish they were nonmonogamous, or the opposite. Whatever it is, it's important to remember that our partners aren't us and they have their own desires and needs for connection that will likely not be the same as ours. ❧ It's also important to remain flexible with one another and with ourselves. People change over time. Perhaps a partner who initially desired sexual relationships may find their desire changing to wanting more emotional bonds. Being flexible with our partners and ourselves helps us to navigate such shifts.

Do your needs for intimacy and connection differ greatly from those of your partners? How do you accept each other's differences?

Keep in mind when making rules and agreements with your partners that the things you want your partner to agree not to do with someone may turn out to be things you want to do with someone in the future.

The boxes we build around others we build around ourselves. An example: The thought of your nesting partner spending a night away from home with someone else fills you with angst, so you push for an agreement of no overnights. Problem solved, right? Sure, until you start dating someone you like and find yourself wanting to spend the night with them. ❦ Often, when considering all of the things our partners can do with others that scare us or feel threatening, we don't stop to think that we may want to do those things with other people too. Wouldn't we want the freedom to do them? How do we want our partners to show up to our desires for our relationships with others? In creating restrictions for our partners to help us feel safe, we create restrictions for ourselves that keep us limited. ❦ This isn't bashing the need for or the practice of rules and agreements in nonmonogamy. Rather, it's an invitation to look at the full picture created when making them. Additionally, this advice won't land the same for poly/mono pairings—those negotiations have an entirely different angle to consider.

Have you ever asked for an agreement or rule to be made only to find yourself wanting to break it later? How did that work out?

While being nonmonogamous enables us to engage in multiple relationships that meet our varying wants and needs, it is also OK to have certain things that you want to exist in all of the relationships you are in.

Often in online nonmonogamy spaces, someone will make a post talking about something that they are missing in a relationship or something that used to exist in a relationship that no longer does. Many people will respond that the poster can still maintain the relationship they have and just go get what they are missing with another person. ❦ While it is true that nonmonogamy allows us the room to have various relationships that fulfill our various wants and needs, it is also true that there may be things that we want in all of the relationships we are in, and when a relationship we are in no longer provides whatever that is, it no longer appeals to us to continue it as it is. ❦ Maybe you want all kink relationships. Maybe you want all of your partners to be social activists because that's important to you. Maybe you want all of your partners to be relationship anarchists or solo-polyamorous. For me, all of my romantic relationships have to have a sexual element. I fully support non-sexual romantic relationships and partnerships, I just don't engage in them personally. ❦ Whatever it is, it's OK to have some relational wants and needs that go across the board.

Do you have relationship needs that are universal for all of your partnerships? What are they?

The more interconnected intimate relationships we engage in, the more the ripple effects of our choices can be felt. Be mindful of the impact your choices have on everyone affected by them, not just the person directly in front of you.

I used to have a standing Wednesday date night with partner. One Wednesday before Thanksgiving, my partner's spouse changed their travel plans to see family for the holiday and arbitrarily canceled my date night with my partner. I was upset because they had made a decision that impacted me and no consideration was made for how I would be affected by it. ❋ Maybe you've chosen to be sexually unbarriered with a new partner. That impacts all partners you're unbarriered with. Maybe you've decided you wish to nest with a new partner. That impacts any partners you're already nested with. Maybe you have decided to stay an extra few days out of town with a partner. That impacts the partner you co-parent with, who is home with the kids while you're away. ❋ When making decisions in nonmonogamy, acknowledge and show care and concern for the folks who are impacted by those choices. If possible, also ask for input from the folks impacted by your choices, not necessarily to decide what your ultimate decisions will be, but to inform your choices. ❋ And if you want to have a nonmonogamous experience in which your choices have minimal impact on folks, set your life up in a way to accomplish that.

What ripple effects have you experienced from your partners' relationships with others? Did they have a significant impact on you?

An important part of improving our relationship to boundaries is changing our perceptions of them. Boundaries are necessary, healthy, caring and a gift to others and to ourselves.

I believe that much of the anxiety and dread that people experience around boundaries has to do with our perceptions of them. We see them as "mean" or "harsh," or we worry that they will hurt the feelings of the people we are setting them with. If we have experienced relationships where our boundaries were not respected, that can shape our understanding too. ❀ If we view boundaries and boundary-setting as drudgery and something to dread, that will influence how we show up to them. If we view boundaries as necessary, healthy and a way to ensure that we are in relationships that feel pleasurable and good for us, that also will impact how we show up to them, both in our attitude to setting them and in our attitude to others setting them with us. ❀ There isn't a single relationship we have that doesn't require the setting of boundaries and the receiving of boundaries and yet we all struggle with this. Changing how we view boundaries shifts our entire relationship with them from something to avoid to something to welcome and embrace.

What is your relationship to boundaries? What feelings come up for you when you think about setting boundaries or receiving a boundary?

Day 120

While it is a good thing to have concern for your metamours, be mindful of being so concerned about their comfort that you end up making yourself uncomfortable. Avoid placing their needs and desires above your own.

Showing compassion and concern for our metamours is helpful in nonmonogamy but when it comes at the expense of your own comfort in your relationship, it isn't sustainable. You do not have to constantly sacrifice yourself, your wants and needs and your relationship with your partner on the altar of the comfort of your metamours. ❁ The most ideal situation is that everyone involved feels as comfortable as possible and also understands that discomfort is at times inevitable and embraces that. Discomfort doesn't always mean that someone needs to change, and it creates opportunities for growth. When you are constantly trying to keep a metamour from being uncomfortable, it removes opportunities for them to grow around your relationship with your partner and will likely cause you to build resentment.

Have you ever sacrificed your comfort in a relationship for the needs of your metamours? If so, how did it make you feel?

A common cause of issues in polyamory is a difference of opinion among partners on what needs to be shared and what doesn't. Having a conversation about disclosure agreements is helpful.

Some partners may want to know when you go on a first date with a person. Some partners may only want to know when someone becomes a partner. Some partners want to know when you begin a sexual relationship with someone new. Some partners will want to know when you say or hear "I love you" with someone. Some partners don't need any of this information. ❧ How much to disclose will vary for each relationship. It will likely also vary for you—your disclosure needs from a nesting partner may be different from someone you don't live with. ❧ Make sure you discuss with each partner what disclosure looks like for that relationship and honor the privacy needs of everyone involved. If you disagree on something that should or shouldn't be shared, try to see if there's a middle ground that makes each person feel acknowledged. ❧ As a side note, you should always share relevant practical and logistical things like what time you plan to be home, when you're bringing someone to your home, if you're spending a large sum of money, etc. with your nesting partner or anyone they affect. The partners you share finances, a home or children with are affected by what you do in more ways than emotionally.

Have you had a conversation on what to disclose with each of your partners? What are some of the disclosure agreements you have made with them?

You can recognize that your partners have the freedom to make whatever choices they wish and also hold that some of these choices may cause you to change or even end your relationship with them. You get to have your hard noes.

We all have things that are hard noes for us. If our partners did these things, it would result in us changing or ending our relationship with them. It's not saying that they can't do the thing, but that they can't do the thing and continue to be with us in the way they currently are. We have a right to name what those things are for us. ❧ That said, some people use this as a tactic for controlling others. Examine your motives. Avoid empty threats and consider if it is truly a hard no. Be prepared for your partner to say, "OK, then we have to end this here." And on the flip side, if you feel like your partner is trying to change or control you with behavior like this, don't succumb to it. You can respond with something like, "It's unfortunate that you feel that way, but this is a choice I'm making, and I understand that you may need to adjust or end our relationship in response to it."

What are some choices that your partners could make that would be hard noes for you?

New challenges in polyamory can seem scary. We don't know how we're going to feel or how much we're going to struggle with. Meeting them with curiosity instead of judgment can help.

Your partner's first date or first overnight with a new connection. Your first trip away from your spouse with a new love. Your first time introducing all of your partners to your family. There are so many examples of new challenges that arise in polyamory that can trigger our fears and anxieties. It helps to approach them, and navigate through them, with curiosity. ❀ Imagine being like a child walking through a new field. What new flowers and plants are you going to see? What sensations will you feel in the grass? What interesting new bugs are you going to uncover digging in the ground? Apply the same approach to challenges in nonmonogamy. When you remain curious, you meet your thoughts and feelings from a place of wonder and a desire to get to know more about them. Consider where they're coming from, what they signify and how to address them. When you approach new things from a space of fear and dread, it makes the process more arduous and dismal. And you can't process thoughts and feelings when you are judging their existence from the door. ❀ Meet yourself with curiosity and wonder, even in the face of hardship or struggle, and you'll keep your relationship to life fresh and new.

Do new situations and challenges in polyamory give you anxiety? What about them causes you to feel uneasy?

Needing reassurance doesn't make you less polyamorous. It makes you human.

I credit Alicia Bunyan Sampson, who blogs as Polyamorous Black Girl, for helping me consider this one. It is human to need reassurance. We need it on our jobs, in our families, in our friend groups. It baffles me that we act like there's something wrong with needing reassurance in our romantic relationships, especially in polyamory. ❧ Nonmonogamy can be very triggering to our personal sensitivities around being worthy of being loved and desired. It is normal to need reassurance from our partners at times and OK to ask for it. To me, the mark of a caring partner is someone who is genuinely concerned about you feeling secure in their regard for you. When my reasonable requests for reassurance are met with resistance or even hostility, that's a red flag. ❧ That said, if you find yourself needing constant reassurance, assess whether it's that your relationships aren't working in a way for you to feel secure in them or if you need to do some deeper work in believing in your self-worth.

Do you feel less suited for nonmonogamy when you are in a space of needing reassurance? What about needing reassurance makes you feel unsuited for nonmonogamy?

It's OK to assert a boundary to not discuss your partners' other relationships. As long as you honor their right to have the relationships, you get to decide how much access you have to them.

It is not immature, childish or unhealthy to ask for this. I'm not referring to wishing to remain completely unaware about a partner's relationship but requesting to have as little exposure as possible to it. ❀ I have had partners who had relationships that bothered me greatly and I felt no qualms about asking them to refrain from sharing information about them with me. I don't owe my partners free range to discuss their relationships with others with me, especially if it's unsettling to my mental or emotional health. As long as I am not interfering in their relationships with others, I feel at peace about it. ❀ This is also why it's important for us to have other people to share with besides our partners, so we aren't burdening them with information they may not want to know simply because we have nowhere else to go with it.

What boundaries do you have around your exposure to your partners' other relationships?

Choosing the right partners is fundamental to polyamorous success. Just because you can date someone, doesn't mean you should.

It took me a long time to realize this. When I first started my nonmonogamous journey, it was like the world of dating opened up for me and I pursued every person I found myself into. It resulted in me finding myself in a state of dating fatigue. ❀ Polyamorous relationships are complex. They have a lot of moving pieces, and I have a lot more considerations than I did when I was dating monogamously. I'm just now learning to slow down with people and feel out the connection before I decide that we should be together in a particular way. Polyamory is challenging enough without the added difficulty of not being intentional about choosing people who are right for you. ❀ When you make good partner choices, the other stuff has a way of working itself out.

How have partner choices impacted your nonmonogamous experience?

Not all breakups come like loud booms, crashing cymbals or symphonies of chaos. Sometimes they are like soft whispers of knowing and releasing.

I gained this insight from a good friend of mine, Quiana Perkins. The ending of my marriage is an example of this. We weren't fighting all the time, or even at all. It wasn't tumultuous. We got along relatively well and we did our best to be kind and gracious to one another. And yet, we were still ending that phase of our relationship. It was hard to reconcile the quietness of it all. ❧ Most of us really don't know how to break up well. Society spends so much time perpetuating the belief that ending a romantic relationship is a catastrophic event, that breaking up means you failed and that relationships that "work" last forever. ❧ I know there are probably people who think polyamory is the cause of my marriage ending. It isn't. If anything, I'm grateful for polyamory because my separation would have been much harder on me if I hadn't developed the relationship tools I needed through practicing nonmonogamy. Truthfully, we had problems long before we became nonmonogamous. It's even possible that we lasted as long as we did *because* we became polyamorous. There might be some alternate reality where we never explored polyamory and we broke up five years sooner. ❧ I chose not to grip tightly, scream and yell or make a scene. I chose to release softly. If your own relationships end, consider doing the same.

How can softness help when a relationship ends?

It's important to get past our hurt from previous relationships so we don't interact with our current partners as if they are the former partners who caused us pain.

Sometimes, something will happen in my current relationships that reminds me of a hurtful event in a former relationship. When that happens, I find myself interacting as if my current partner is my former one. ❧ But they're not. They're a different person, and so am I. If I stay stuck in hurt from the past, I can never be present in the current reality and I can't be present with who my partner is or who I am. I'll just keep reliving the past, both as I relate to others and as I relate to myself.

In what ways do you relive former relationship pains in your current relationships?

Our partners can make choices that feel deeply personal and like they didn't consider us or our feelings at all, but they likely weren't trying to hurt us. It's more likely that they were just trying to fulfill themselves.

One of my all-time favorite movies is *Doctor Strange*. There's a conversation between Dr. Strange and the Ancient One in which the Ancient One says, "Arrogance and fear still keep you from learning the simplest and most significant lesson of all. It's not about you." ✤ I am not denying the human capacity to intentionally cause harm, even to someone we love. And I'm also not advocating for being OK with partners who are completely inconsiderate and self-focused. But if that is the case in your relationships, the issue still isn't your partner's choices, but the fact that you believe that you have a partner who has intentional disregard for you or tries to harm you and cause you pain. ✤ One of the best pieces of polyamory advice I have ever received is, "Assume good intent about your partners." If you can honestly say that your partner cares for you and they have not shown themselves to be a person who intentionally tries to hurt you, why would that have changed? Perhaps it hasn't, even if it feels like that is what's going on. ✤ Our partners are people just like us. They're trying to do the best they can to fulfill themselves. It's good to remember that.

Is it hard for you to not take your partners' choices personally? What about their choices feels personal to you?

Asking our partners to alter their relationships with others because we are having issues in our relationship with them is like asking a friend to stop hanging out with other friends until they fix an issue they have with us.

We don't do this in other relationship structures. If you had an issue with a friend you needed to work out, you wouldn't ask them to halt or cease all friendships in the meantime. ❧ Frankly, this occurs disproportionately to solo-polyamorous and single folks who date married or nested folks with "primary" partnerships. Some people find it totally acceptable to make a request for their spouse to pause or end their other relationships if there's an issue in the primary partnership, but it usually doesn't work the other way around if there's an issue in the secondary relationship. ❧ All relationships have rough patches, whether they're nonmonogamous or not. But it can be difficult to watch our partner at ease with someone when we are struggling in our relationship with them. However, dealing with that by seeking to control the other relationship rarely works. Rather, it usually breeds resentment. ❧ Focus on what you and your partner need to do, independent of what they have going on with others. You need to learn how to have a good relationship while you have other partners and also how to work out issues while you have other partners.

Have you ever tried to limit a partner's relationship with someone else because you were struggling in your relationship with your partner? If so, what were you trying to accomplish by doing this? Did it work?

Wading through the messier parts of your emotions before bringing them to your partners cuts down on processing time. Sit with yourself, journal or talk to a trusted friend or counselor.

Emotions can be messy, sticky and muddy. And the reality is that our partners aren't always capable or willing to go through our entire process with us, especially if we are someone who has large emotions or our partners have a lower bandwidth for emotions than we do. Additionally, there are parts of our process that have nothing to do with them or that might be harmful for them to be involved with, especially if we are initially upset with them. ❀ Learning to do some of your emotional processing "off-stage" from your partners allows you to come to them with a much more concise message that is easier to digest and respond to. ❀ Sitting with yourself, writing out your feelings or talking to someone you trust are excellent ways to get through the emotional debris so that when you address your partners, you have identified the essence of what is most important for them to know.

How do you process your emotions on your own or away from your partners?

Day 132

The best kinds of loves are not the ones that seek to fill in the broken parts of ourselves or try to heal us but the ones that seek to lovingly hold and support us as we fill in those broken parts and heal ourselves.

I can't heal you and you can't heal me, but we can support one another as we seek to heal ourselves alongside one another. ❧ A good friend said this to me: "I can only be your question, not your answer."

How do your partners create a supportive environment for you to heal? How do you create that for them?

When we get triggered, we can experience myriad emotions all at once. You don't need to process them all at the same time. Just start with the one that needs the most attention and love.

Often, I face a challenging situation in polyamory and it's so complex that I experience an array of emotions simultaneously. It can be overwhelming at times. ✿ I've learned to take a step back and focus on the emotion that is strongest. I look at the part of myself that needs the most attention, compassion and love. The other feelings will also receive their care in time. It's important when we're triggered not to try to take on too much at once but to be intentional and patient with ourselves as we process.

What tools you have developed to quiet your emotions when they are all going off at once?

When seeking to establish closer relationships with your metamours, try looking for things you connect on aside from having a mutual partner.

Some of my favorite people are former metamours. Our relationships with each other have endured long after we stopped having a mutual partner. That's because they are people who I genuinely enjoy as human beings, not just because we were with the same person. ❀ Basing my relationship with someone solely on their connection to someone else I'm connected to has no appeal to me. I'd rather bond with them on an individual level. Our relationships with our partner may change, but the one we have with each other doesn't have to be affected by that. It's good to seek out other ways to appreciate your metamours apart from them just being your partner's partner. ❀ Additionally, make sure to respect the level of closeness they wish to have with you. My best meta relationships happened naturally and didn't feel forced by any party.

What do you have in common with your metamours besides having the same partner?

When we've been with a partner for a while, we can resent the ways they show up in newer relationships because we can see them exhibiting growth to other partners that we didn't experience.

When my husband and I entered into nonmonogamy, we had been married for nine years. We had both gone through a lot of growth together. It used to really bother me watching how he showed up to his other partners from a more mature space. It felt like the newer partners were reaping the benefit of years of my blood, sweat and tears. I am also certain that he can say the same thing about his experience of watching me with my newer partners—I show up far more emotionally healthy to them than I did when he and I first got together. ❧ It's not fair to hold your partner to who they used to be to you when they are interacting with others. People are allowed to grow. It's also possible that their other partners interact with them in ways that bring out a different version of them than you did. Rather than resent your partner or their other partners, work on healing the damage that may have occurred in your relationship before either of you knew better.

Do you struggle to watch your partners exhibit growth toward others that you didn't get to experience until later in your relationship? What makes accepting their growth as it relates to others hard for you?

Judging our partners' emotions makes it hard for them to be emotionally vulnerable with us. The same goes for us when we judge ourselves for our emotions.

Imagine this: You and a new partner have decided to become sexually intimate. On your first time with them, you take your clothes off and they finally see you naked. The first thing they say when they see your body is, "Why does your chest look like that? It shouldn't look that way," or "Your skin is the wrong color on your thighs," or "Your body shouldn't look like that." How would you feel? Would you wish to go forward with sex with them? Would you continue to want a sexual relationship with them? ❀ It's the same thing when our partners are emotionally "naked" with us. When they bare their emotional bodies to us, responding with judgment and scorn doesn't help them feel safe to be vulnerable with us in that way. Yes, they have a responsibility to express those emotions in a healthy way and to also acknowledge that their emotions aren't an excuse for problematic behavior, but if they are doing that work, responding with empathy and compassion goes much further than judging them for normal human feelings. ❀ And in the same vein, when we judge ourselves for our emotions, it's like standing naked in front of a mirror criticizing every part of our body that we don't like. That makes it hard for us to show up to being emotionally vulnerable with ourselves.

Do you judge your partners or yourself in moments of emotional vulnerability? In what ways?

You can have ten partners and still find yourself feeling lonely. Polyamory is not a substitute for learning how to be with yourself.

Once, my partner had to go out of town unexpectedly to help his other partner move. That same weekend, my other partner was spending the weekend with his other partner. I had a few things happen during that time that were emotionally challenging for me and neither of my partners were available because they were with their other loves. I had to handle my emotions by myself. ❀ The reality is that no matter how many partners you have, you are still going to have times where none of them are available for you. You need to be able to sit with yourself and your own company, learn how to self-soothe and be comfortable being with you. The relationship you have with yourself is your most important one, and polyamory isn't a cure for loneliness. Learn to be just as present in your relationship with yourself as you are in your relationships with others.

How do you cultivate the relationship you have with yourself?

Engaging in polyamory can show us what we definitely don't want in relationships, but it can also show us what we do want, and sometimes it highlights that the relationships we are in are lacking.

People sometimes enter polyamory in a relationship that seems good on paper—or good enough—and then realize that it isn't as fulfilling as they thought it was. When they become aware of the possibilities of what relationships can look and feel like for them, they have new perspective. I hear things like, "I just thought this is what all relationships were like" or "My relationship was better than most of the ones I saw around me" from people who are realizing they were happy enough but not truly fulfilled. ❧ In nonmonogamy, you can meet people who show you that the things you thought you had to compromise on are actually available, and it can make you reevaluate how you want *all* of your relationships to be. That can be scary both for yourself and for your partners. ❧ There's a difference between being "happy" with your relationships and being truly fulfilled by them.

Are your relationships fulfilling for you? What does having a fulfilling relationship mean to you?

Day 139

We are not entitled to our partners' emotional processes or them sharing every emotion we want them to when we want them to. Emotional consent and emotional autonomy are important.

I used to call myself the Emotional Linebacker. If there was an emotional situation happening, I wanted my partners to talk about their feelings exactly when, how and if I wanted them to. I would bum-rush my partner with "feelings talk." It wasn't a good practice to have. Yes, it meant that things always got dealt with in a timely fashion, but it didn't honor my partner's emotional process and their sovereignty over that. ❧ Today, my partners get to choose which emotions they share with me and when they feel safe enough to share them. They also get to keep some things to themselves. I needed to learn to ask them if they wish to share with me, accept when they don't and allow them the freedom to process in their own way (so long as their process isn't abusive or harmful to themselves or to me). ❧ Don't forget that our partners also get to feel what they feel—we can't dictate that.

Do you feel entitled to all of your partners' emotions or feel like your partners are entitled to all of yours? How do you honor emotional privacy and consent in your relationships?

We do no one, least of all ourselves, any favors by pretending to feel a way we don't truly feel. Being honest about your genuine feelings is the best way for you to honor yourself.

When I first started polyamory, I would see all of these posts in groups about compersion and how it was the best way to feel in order to live nonmonogamously. Like many people who begin this journey, I began to elevate this emotion even though I had no experience with it. That led to me pretending to feel happy when my partner began interacting with others because that's what I thought I was supposed to be feeling. It never worked and, more often than not, went really badly. I learned pretty quickly that pretending to be "better" at this than I actually was wasn't good for anyone, least of all myself. ❦ Be honest (with kindness) about your genuine feelings. It doesn't help your partners for you to pretend to be in a space that you aren't in. They can't support feelings that they don't know you're having. Personally, I would rather have someone's authentic unhappiness than someone's inauthentic happiness.

What are some ways you think are "right" to feel and ways you think are "wrong" to feel? Why do you believe that there are right and wrong ways to feel?

Day 141

Our partners have limits to how much they wish to know of our discomfort about their other relationships, especially since those relationships bring them joy.

While we don't have to be overflowing with joy about our partners' relationships with others if that's not what we are genuinely feeling, being consistently negative and difficult about them because of our uncomfortable feelings isn't helpful, either. Most people feel bothered when people they care about can't or won't share in their joy about something in their life. And even though our partners may desire to support us through those uncomfortable feelings, they still have limits to how much support they can offer or how willing they are to hear us talk about something that brings them joy in a negative way. ❀ I'm not saying that you shouldn't be honest about your feelings with your partners, but try to be concise. Learn to process your feelings internally as much as you can, and develop a network of close friends and confidants who can help you wade through some of the stickier parts of your emotions.

How does it make you feel when your partners are consistently negative about your relationships with others?

When a partner violates a relationship agreement, part of the work that needs to be done is examining the agreement.

Was the agreement reasonable in the first place? Did our partner agree to it under duress? Was it vague enough to be misinterpreted? It's not always as simple as "they did a bad thing and violated my trust." ❃ When someone violates a relationship agreement, it's easy to feel victimized by the perceived betrayal. But if you can set that aside for a minute, you might find that it isn't as simple as "my partner did me wrong." These things are always more complex than they appear on the surface.

Have you ever violated a relationship agreement? If so, why?

Make sure to ask any partnered people you date what relationship agreements they have with other partners early on. It's not uncommon to find yourself subject to a relationship restriction you weren't aware of and wouldn't have consented to.

It's important to ask questions early on, especially if you are single or solo-poly. It's not uncommon for folks to find themselves involved with a person and have already developed feelings for them only to find themselves subject to a relationship restriction that they weren't aware of and didn't consent to. Partnered people often make relationship agreements for other relationships without the input of the people affected by those agreements. Ask the questions.

Have you ever found yourself subject to a relationship restriction you didn't know was in place when you agreed to the relationship? If so, what impact did that have on you?

If your partner is reasonably asking for reassurance and you have the ability to offer it to them, doing so is an easy and loving way you can give to your partner. You may not understand why they need it but recognize that they are struggling and your reassurance can put their mind and heart at ease.

Sometimes your partner just needs to hear that you are still into them, especially if they are trying to handle you being into others. I'm not talking about if they are acting out because they need reassurance, but when they come to you vulnerably. Don't treat them like they are being silly or like it's a burden to you to reassure them. I'm sure they are already worried about those things in their mind. It's hard to be vulnerable and ask for reassurance.

Do you struggle to give your partners reassurance when they ask for it? How does it make you feel when your requests for reassurance are met with resistance?

When you find yourself feeling triggered by what a partner is doing, assess what is really bothering you first. Often, it's not the initial trigger that's the issue but what's underneath it. Take the time to dig beyond what's on the surface.

I often find that when I'm feeling triggered by something my partners are doing, the first thoughts and feelings aren't the most accurate indicators of what is really going on with me. When I take the time to examine what I'm feeling, I uncover much deeper emotions. It's asking myself things like, "Am I really upset that my partner went on a date to see a horror film with their new partner or am I feeling threatened because their new partner likes horror films and I don't?" ❀ If I approach my partners for support with only the surface thoughts and feelings, I will likely experience a temporary soothing of my problem, but the underlying issues would go unaddressed and it would just be a matter of time before they resurface. Taking the time to peel back the layers and get to the root of my emotions helps me to get what I deeply need in order to heal and move forward.

What tools do you use to effectively examine your emotions?

No amount of polyamory advice will work if you are being treated poorly by your partners. Ask yourself if your issues stem from things you need to work on or if they are signs that you aren't being treated well and need to reevaluate your relationships.

My advice almost always comes from the assumption that people are in mostly healthy relationships with decent people who are doing their best to treat them well. None of the tips I give will be useful to people who are in relationships with partners who are abusive or who are unconcerned about their relationships being mutually fulfilling. ❧ Sometimes, it's not about folks needing to do more internal work to fix the issue. Sometimes folks are simply in bad relationships with people who aren't good for them and that's what needs to change.

Have you ever stayed too long in a relationship that wasn't good for you by trying to work on yourself more? If so, what was the result?

The labels we attach to our relationships also come with our beliefs about what that label means and we often assume our partners share the same beliefs, but they may not. "Partner" to you and "partner" to them can mean very different things.

It's important to have clear conversations with your partners and potential partners around what it means for you when a person has a particular label in your life. We often have ideas and assumptions about how a person "should" show up based on a label they carry in our lives and then end up breaking our own hearts when they don't live up to our expectations. ❀ Is it really that they don't love or care for you, or is it that they didn't know you expected them to behave a certain way because of who they are to you?

What does the word "partner" mean to you?
What expectations do you have of a person
holding the title of "partner" in your life?

Learn to focus on quality of care rather than quantity of care. I have found that when I focus less on how much I am getting from my partners and instead focus on how good it is, I don't need as much as I thought I did.

Consider this: If you went to a physical therapist three times a week but only noticed minimal improvement and then switched to a physical therapist you saw once a week but noticed a very marked improvement to your condition, which experience would you be happier with? ❀ When I learned to focus on the quality of care in my relationships and less on the quantity, it made making room for my partners to have other people in their lives romantically a lot easier and I found that I didn't "need" as much care as I thought I did.

What does quality care in your relationships look like for you?

You can't change people and you can't be in a relationship with who you wish they were. You must be with who they are.

I ask myself: "If this person stayed exactly as they are today for the rest of their life, can I accept that?" If the answer is yes, I continue in my relationship with them and make peace with who they are—both the things about them that I enjoy and the things about them that I struggle to enjoy. If the answer is no, I explore what options are available to me to help me accept who they are, be that changing or ending my relationship with them or asking them if there are considerations they are able and willing to make to accommodate me. My answer to this question, however, is never "I need to figure out how to change them." ❦ You also can't separate a person from their circumstances. I often hear, "So and so would be great if it wasn't for ____," but a person's circumstances also inform who they are and how they are able to show up.

Do you enter relationships with folks wishing to change things about who they are? How does it feel when people attempt to change you?

**It's impossible to set things up so that you always
have a date when your partners have dates or an
overnight when your partners have an overnight.
Release the idea that you have to be doing the same
things at the same time as your partners to be OK.**

Early in my polyamorous journey, I was an "even Stevens"
person. I always wanted to go tit for tat with my partners. If
they had a date, I had to have a date set up. One weekend
when one of my partners was away with another partner,
I tried so hard to set up something with someone else
and I couldn't make it happen. I was upset about this and
sitting with my emotions about it when I heard a small
inner voice say to me, "But did you die?" I didn't. And I
realized in that moment that while I was uncomfortable,
I got through it and was OK. I broke the need to be
matching my partners' interactions with others with my own
interactions with others. ❧ Even with the most concerted
of efforts, it's impossible to always be doing something
with someone else when your partners are doing things
with others. It's also exhausting to even try to make that
happen. Release the need to even the score with your
partners. It's not a competition.

Are you an "even Stevens" person in your relationships? If so,
why does ensuring that everything is equal matter to you?

Release the need to have your monogamous friends and family understand your nonmonogamy. It's OK if they don't get it, and you don't need their permission to live your authentic truth. Embrace your understanding and affirmation of yourself.

In a perfect world, our families and friends would be supportive of our polyamory and even if they didn't understand it, they would want us to be happy and making choices that are authentic to how we want to live and love. We don't live in a perfect world, though, and sometimes that means our loved ones can't support or understand our choice to live a polyamorous life. In those instances, we must remember that we don't need them to understand us as long as *we* understand us. If polyamory is what is best for you, then that is what matters. ❀ I believe that it is not my job to make people understand me. It is my job simply to be me. ❀ I also want to add that your friends and family not getting you being polyamorous is no excuse for them being disrespectful to you about it. If they are unkind, judgmental or disrespectful to you about it, you have every right to address that and create boundaries between you and them about it.

Do you find it difficult or hurtful when your family and friends aren't supportive of and understanding about you being polyamorous? If so, why is their acceptance important to you? What does it mean to you?

Resist the urge to date people because you're lonely, you don't want to be the partner without another partner, or you don't believe you can find what you really want in a relationship. Relationships feel best when the primary motivation for being with a person is simply that you want to be with them.

I've made a personal commitment to myself that I'm going to stop involving myself in relationships where my motivation for being with the person is anything other than I simply want to be with them. Dating someone because I'm lonely, in response to my partners having other partners or because I don't think I can find what I'm truly looking for has never yielded fulfilling results. It's treating people as objects and not as people. ❀ When I believe that someone is interacting with me for any other reason than the fact that they desire to be with me, that doesn't feel good. I want to treat people how I want to be treated so I make sure I am checking in with myself and my motivations for being with someone.

Have you ever been in a relationship where you believed that the person wasn't with you for you? If so, how did you feel in that relationship?

When feeling anxiety about all the ways things can go wrong in polyamory, pause and think of all the ways things can go right.

"What if they try to steal my partner?" can become "What if they become an awesome new metamour?" "What if I don't find anyone I can have the relationship I want to have with?" can become "What if I meet several people I can be in authentic relationships with?" "What if my partner has a better time with their other partner than they do with me?" can become "What if my partner has a great time and feels so happy and fulfilled that they come back to me even more excited about our relationship?" ❧ If we're examining the possibilities, why not examine all of them, especially the ones that are positive?

How can you spin your negative thoughts into positive ones?

Polyamory does not mean being OK with everything. If you're uncomfortable with something, that's valid, and it's OK to ask for support.

It's OK to bring your feelings of discomfort to your partners and ask them for support. For example, it's OK to be upset if it's your birthday and your partner decides to keep their standard date night with another partner instead of spending it with you. It's also OK to ask your partner if they can reschedule their date night so you can spend your birthday together. If they choose not to, it's OK to be upset about that. None of that would make you "bad" at polyamory. ❧ I reject the notions that you should be OK with anything your partners wish to do with others, that you should never ask them to help you as you deal with your discomfort and that any discomfort or need for support is an indicator that you aren't "good" at this. If you are honoring their autonomy, requesting and not demanding their support and not making them responsible for your feelings, it's OK to ask them to work with you on ways they can be considerate of your discomfort.

Have you ever pretended to be OK with something in polyamory when you really weren't? If so, what influenced you to do so?

Day 155

Have the courage to check your dating preferences and see if they are products of societal beliefs about which individuals are deserving of desire.

Desirability politics play a major role in our love and relationship decisions. This refers to the level to which someone is seen as desirable based on factors such as race and ethnicity, gender, economic and social class, sexual orientation, body size, whether they are cisgender or transgender and whether they are disabled. Our dating and relationship preferences are heavily influenced by societal bias against folks who are marginalized and those who fall outside of cisgender, heterosexual, white, able-bodied, thin, affluent identity lines. ❧ Dr. Liz Powell explained this succinctly on Twitter in 2019, saying, "Your preferences can be, and likely are, a product of your culture. Which means they are likely sexist, ableist, racist, colorist, sizeist, homophobic, cissexist, etc. You totally get to *date* whoever you want. *And* your preferences aren't magic, they came from somewhere. If you aren't willing to examine and explore your preferences I can pretty much guarantee that there's societal bullshit in there creating them for you."

Have you examined your dating preferences to see if they are the products of any societal biases? How have you had your attractions challenged?

Day 156

When you find yourself comparing your relationship with your partners to their relationships with others, remind yourself of the unique ways your partners love you.

It is human to compare, so why judge myself for being human? Instead, when I find myself comparing, I develop tools to address it. I remind myself of how awesome I am and I also ask my partners to tell me all the ways they appreciate me specifically so I have things to think back on to counteract my negative thoughts. ❀ When you find yourself comparing yourself to your partners' other partners, try reminding yourself of the ways that you uniquely bring value to their lives. It's not a competition to be the person our partners like the most.

What tools have you developed to combat negative comparisons?

Our partners are allowed to end their romantic connection to us at will. They aren't obligated to be romantic with us after they no longer wish to be simply because that's what we want. Letting go hurts, but holding on to what is long gone hurts more.

You can't fight for a relationship by yourself, especially if someone is clearly indicating they no longer wish to be with you in a particular way. Holding on to what no longer exists is like holding on to a blade. The tighter you grip it, the more damage you do to yourself. The sooner you let go, the sooner you can heal.

What helps you to let go when a relationship ends?

Sometimes, you find yourself in a space where you are cheering for your partner and their relationship wins while you are disappointed for yourself and your relationship losses. It's a skill to be able to hold both.

It can be hard to be supportive and encouraging and happy for our partners experiencing love wins when we are experiencing love losses or even just wanting some wins of our own. ❧ A friend once told me to remember that the pendulum of life always swings back in the other direction eventually. I ask myself, "How would I want my partner to behave toward me if they were in my position?" I also allow myself to be both happy for them and sad for me. The presence of one set of emotions doesn't cancel out the other. ❧ I also communicate what I'm feeling with my partners and ask for reassurance and support. I say, "I'm glad you're having a positive experience in your relationships but I'm struggling because I'm not having the same. Can you remind me that I'm worthy of relationship wins and that my time will come, too?"

How do you behave toward your partners when things are going well in their other relationships while you are struggling in your own?

Intimacy requires vulnerability, and vulnerability requires safety. If you find yourself struggling to engage in intimate connection, ask yourself where you are feeling unsafe and why.

This is a simple and straightforward concept, but one that people struggle with. You can't experience intimacy without vulnerability, and you can't be truly vulnerable in a situation where you don't feel safe. Intimacy means connection. Vulnerability means letting your guard down. If you feel unsafe, the last thing you will want to do is expose yourself by taking off your armor. ❦ Many things can contribute to not feeling safe. Past hurts, a person's behavior, even our present life circumstances can all contribute to how safe we feel to be vulnerable to others. When you're struggling to experience intimacy, examining where you're not feeling safe can provide you with the answers you need to change your situation and put you back on the road to connection.

What helps you feel safe to be vulnerable in a relationship?

Day 160

It is OK to decide that you have a limited capacity for processing your partners' difficult emotions about polyamory with them or even to decide you have no desire to do so.

There is nothing wrong with someone understanding their own emotional capacity and deciding that they have limited ability to process their partners' difficult emotions with them, or even to decide it's just not something they wish to do. They may be willing to respond to requests that arise as a result of those emotions or to offer reassurances needed as a result of those emotions, but decide that the process of getting to the root of their partners' emotions is something they aren't willing or capable of doing. ✻ This does not make someone bad at polyamory or cold-hearted or self-absorbed. We all make choices about how we wish to be in relationships in accordance with what we are capable and willing to do. If you are not willing or able to process difficult emotions about polyamory, inform your partners and potential partners and seek to form relationships with people who either feel similarly about this or who are less emotional individuals so you are in alignment with one another.

What difficult emotions are you willing to process with your partners about nonmonogamy? Are there any difficult emotions you aren't willing to process with your partners?

Day 161

Sometimes we are so focused on being a good partner to all of our partners that we forget to be a good partner to ourselves. You are in a relationship with yourself, too. Be a good partner to you.

Make sure you are showing up for yourself. Most relationships require some measure of sacrifice, but you can only be a good partner to others from a space of being good to yourself. Don't sacrifice yourself to the point of injury trying to be "good" to others.

How do you nurture your relationship with yourself?

Equality in all your relationships isn't the goal in polyamory. Each relationship has a different set of needs.

You wouldn't apply the exact same care to a toddler as you would a teen. Different people have different needs and when we focus on trying to make sure we are treating our partners equally, we can end up not meeting the individual needs of each of our partners. While the standard of care should be the same, the kinds of care we give to our partners should be specific to what they each value about being in relationship with us. ❧ The goal is to ensure that each relationship you're in has what it uniquely needs in order to thrive. Focus on equity of care and not equality of care.

What are some needs you can identify that are unique to each of your partners?

Our partners don't have the same triggers that we do and thus don't have the same sensitivities. Often, when we think our partners are being insensitive, it's because they don't have the same sensitivities and aren't aware of yours.

Imagine that you post a picture of yourself and one of your partners on Facebook. You fix the settings on the picture so that your other partners can't see it because it's a trigger for you when your partners post pics with their other partners on social media. Then one of your partners posts a pic of them and another partner on their page. ❧ You get upset. You say to yourself, "That's so insensitive! I always make sure that they don't have to see my photos of my other partners so why don't they do that for me?" But they didn't ask you to do that because it doesn't bother them for you to post pics. It bothers you. And you likely didn't tell them it's something that bothers you or ask them to change their settings on those posts so you don't see them. ❧ Sometimes, your partners aren't being insensitive, they're just being themselves.

What are some things you are sensitive about that your partners are not?

Day 164

Trust that your partners can manage their own emotions even when they are difficult or uncomfortable. If you pull back on doing things every time your partner expresses discomfort with your choices, you rob them of their opportunity to grow.

Your partners are grown adults who agreed to be non-monogamous. Discomfort will happen. I'm not saying be completely insensitive to their feelings but that leaning into the discomfort of polyamory and working through it is how we grow. If your partner expresses discomfort about what you're doing, have empathy for that while maintaining the choices you've made. Don't cut off opportunities for them to grow.

Do you pull back on the choices you've made when your partners express being uncomfortable with them? If so, why?

Day 165

For some people, the nonmonogamous community
is their first experience interacting with queer people,
trans folks, people of other ethnicities and cultures
or neurodivergent and disabled folks. Take time
to educate yourself on these identities so you can
be sensitive and check your own privileges.

Talking to the cis-hets, the able-bodied, the white folks.
In this age of readily accessible information, it is time to
stop using the excuse of "I didn't know." ❧ Privilege is
assuming that all spaces are safe spaces because they
are safe for you. Learn to be mindful of other people,
including those who are marginalized, and take the time
to discover what their experiences of moving through the
world are. This will help you to show up well when you
encounter them and help avoid you burdening them with
"having grace" with you and educating you.

Have you taken the initiative to educate yourself on marginalized
communities you aren't a part of? What have you learned?

Whether or not you date monogamous people is a personal choice but when dating as a polyamorous person, it is best to be up-front as early as possible about being nonmonogamous so there is no expectation of exclusivity from you.

The sooner you tell someone you're polyamorous, the better. Remember, we want people to accept us for who we truly are. And not being up-front about being nonmonogamous can lead your dating prospects to feel misled or lied to. It's a conversation that should be had right away.

How soon do you tell a potential interest that you are nonmonogamous? Do you experience fear when doing so?

Our partners usually don't wish to keep things from us, but our reactions to their sharing with us can make it harder for them to be open. Examine yourself to see if you create a safe space for transparency.

In the past, I would have such emotional reactions to what my partner shared about their other relationships that it made it much harder for them to be fully transparent with me. I'm not saying that you should deny your genuine emotions, but learn how to express them in ways that encourage a safe space for your partners to continue to be transparent and share with you.

Has a partner ever had a strong emotional reaction to your transparency about relationships with others? Did those reactions make it more difficult for you to continue to be transparent with them? How did you address that?

Some people take issue with their partners and their friends dating each other and others do not. Neither way is right or wrong, just different. Discuss your views about this with your partners and potential partners.

Personally, I don't like my partners dating my friends and I generally avoid my friends' partners as dating options. I have had partners, however, who didn't feel the same way about this. I also have friends who don't take issue with dating the partners of their friends. I used to view it as disloyalty to me when my friends and partners wanted to date one another. Now, it's just something that makes me uncomfortable but I don't judge them as bad people because of it. ❧ Don't assume that your partners or your friends feel the same as you do about this, either in the positive or the negative. You may like a friend of your partner and not pursue them because you think your partner won't like it, but they could actually be fine with it. You might begin dating your partner's friend and think that your partner will be excited about it, only to find out that they have an issue with it. It's better to talk about these things with an open mind and understand that the viewpoint you hold about it is only your own.

How do you feel about your partners
and friends dating each other?

Day 169

Forgive yourself for times where you made mistakes or didn't behave how you would have wished to. Polyamory isn't always easy. We all have growing to do, and mistakes are occasions for learning.

We must learn to forgive ourselves for the times when we have "failed" because even failure is a lesson. And we can't move past our mistakes to learn from them and grow if we keep beating ourselves up about them and wrapping ourselves in shame. ❧ Forgive yourself for the past you, celebrate yourself for the present you who has grown from that place and look forward to the future you who will be even more amazing.

What are some past mistakes that you
need to forgive yourself for?

Learn to differentiate between jealousy and envy. Jealousy is feeling threatened by another person or relationship. Envy is wanting something that someone else has. It's an important distinction when trying to navigate your emotions.

Jealousy: "My partner has a new partner who I perceive is more attractive than me. I'm jealous because I'm worried that my partner feels that way too and will want them more than me because of it." ❧ Envy: "My partner has a new partner who is long distance and they get to spend weekends together in new places, something my partner and I don't get to do as often." ❧ Each of these emotions has a different response. They may feel similar, but they are different and the support we need to navigate them will be different. Learn to differentiate between the two.

What things do you feel jealousy about?
What things do you feel envious of?

It's OK to decide that polyamory isn't for you and to return to monogamy. Just like monogamy isn't for everyone, neither is nonmonogamy. It's not a failure to change your mind about it.

If you find yourself continuing to struggle and polyamory just isn't getting any easier or more fulfilling, it could be that maybe you're a monogamous person and aren't allowing yourself to be that. It takes just as much courage to walk away from nonmonogamy as it does to walk into it. Grant yourself the permission to change your mind.

Do you question your ability or desire to live polyamorously? When do those doubts come up most for you?

When you feel jealousy or envy, try to shift your focus from the discomfort you are feeling to the benefit your partners receive from enjoying others. It can help you to focus less on yourself and more on your desire for your partners to have things that bring them joy.

This one comes from a personal story. My long-distance partner, his other partner and I used to meet up on Zoom every Sunday with some friends. One Sunday, my partner and his partner were on the Zoom chat from the same place because they were spending time together. I felt a little envious—not because I have an issue with them being together, but because one of the things I struggle with in my relationship with him is the distance we are from each other. ❀ I was managing my emotions, but then my partner mentioned that his partner grabbed him to get him out of the house and lift his spirits because he was going through something particularly saddening. I felt gratitude that she was able to do that and that he was being supported by someone who loves him. I still felt my little twinge of envy, but the reframing of the situation helped to assuage the feelings. ❀ When you're feeling jealousy or envy, try thinking of the benefit for your partner instead of what it's taking from you. As a person who loves your partner, it's good to remind yourself that you want them to have good things and be happy.

How can you shift your feelings of jealousy to think about what benefits your partners receive when they are happy and able to love freely?

Your "truth" doesn't always have to be something you're proud of for you to embrace it. Sometimes it's childish, ugly, humiliating, angry—something human. Allow yourself your humanity, both darkness and light.

Sometimes, our truths about our feelings in nonmonogamy or what motivated our behaviors feel small, petty, insecure or childish. It can be hard to admit those things to others and to ourselves. Allow yourself to be human. That's part of you, too.

Do you judge yourself for your truths, especially when you are feeling discomfort or pain? What are some truths you find hard to embrace about yourself?

"Polyamorous" does not mean "progressive" or "evolved." The polyamory community is not free from things such as racism, sexism, homophobia, transphobia, classism, fatphobia and ableism. Don't be surprised if you encounter them.

I can't tell you how many times I've heard of a person being surprised that they encountered one or more of these biases in the polyamory community. There's a misguided belief that polyamorous people are somehow more "evolved" than people who don't practice nonmonogamy. Practicing polyamory doesn't automatically mean a person is progressive. It simply means that they engage in multiple romantic relationships. ❀ Just like there are all kinds of monogamous people, there are all kinds of polyamorous people.

Do you hold folks in the polyamorous community to a higher standard than you do people who don't practice polyamory? Why or why not?

Couples who are too "coupled" can struggle in polyamory. Even if you both are with the same person, you will each still have to develop an individual relationship with that person. Develop your individuality.

If you and your partner are wrapped up too tightly in one another, you're going to struggle with maintaining partnerships because there literally won't be any room for anyone else. In polyamory, couples usually feel themselves "separate" from being "one flesh" to being two individuals who are in a relationship with each other. It can feel scary but it's necessary.

How do you work to develop an identity separate from that of your partners?

Have conversations with your partners about what communication looks like when you're away with other partners for an extended period of time. People have different ideas about this and it takes time and effort to find a rhythm that works.

I like daily communication with my partners, even when they are with someone else. One of my former partners could go days without talking to a partner. When they began having out-of-town loves whom they saw for days at a time, it was hard for us and it took some time for us to find a balance of communication that didn't leave me feeling like they forgot about me and didn't leave them feeling like they were being taken out of the moment with their other partners. ❧ Have conversations about communication expectations, understand that your partners may have different (but not wrong) ideas about what that looks like and work toward solutions that honor who each of you are and how each of you wish to communicate. Ask for what you need and be reasonable. It is not reasonable to expect your partner to be available to talk every moment you want them to when they are with someone else but I also think it is not reasonable to expect your partner to be OK with not hearing from you at all for three or four days. Balance is key and is also subjective.

How do you desire to communicate when you or your partners are with others?

It is possible to make your partner's life so miserable because of a connection they have that you don't like that they feel forced to end it to preserve the peace. Be mindful of controlling your partner's relationship choices in this way.

Veto agreements are a hot topic in the polyamorous community. A veto agreement is an agreement between partners in which each has the power to "veto" or say no to their partner's dating prospects or other partners. Some folks have explicit veto agreements that they have created together. Others may not have a veto agreement but make their partner's life so difficult about choices they don't like that they might as well have one. I call this a backdoor veto. You are giving your partner the freedom to be with whomever they choose but not giving them peace about those choices. ❀ I struggled with a few of the partner choices that one of my former partners made and I did not respond well to their relationships. I made it very clear that I did not like their relationships and it was so exhausting for my partner to have to deal with my emotions that it made my partner feel like it wasn't worth the trouble to essentially fight with me to have those relationships. I had to work on that. ❀ We may not always like who our partners choose, but we can respect their right to autonomy in their choices.

Have you ever found a partner's choice of partner difficult? If so, what did you find most difficult about them being connected to someone you didn't like?

Polyamorous relationships are complex and are affected by more variables than monogamous relationships. Simply having romantic feelings for a person isn't enough to cover a multitude of incompatibilities.

Polyamorous relationships have a lot of moving pieces and more considerations than monogamous relationships, in my opinion. Having romantic feelings for a person isn't enough to make a relationship work and I find this to be especially true in polyamory. ❀ You don't need to pursue everyone you experience an attraction to or have chemistry with. Take the time to see if you are compatible in other areas, such as polyamorous philosophy, relationship capacity, core values, etc.

How do you know a person will be compatible with you?

My partners having partners who stand in stark contrast to me can often trigger insecurity and fear. It helps me to remind myself that I enjoy variety and it stands to reason that my partners do too.

I date people who are wildly different from each other and value all of them, yet I struggle to understand this when it's the other way around. I remind myself that I like hot and cold tea. Both beverages have value to me in their differences. I find that having practical concepts to relate my emotions to helps me work with them.

Do you feel insecure when your partners have partners who are drastically different from you? What particular differences cause you to feel insecure?

Day 180

All of my relationships do not look the same but they feel the same in that I feel safe, valued, considered and healthy in all of them. Check the temperature of your relationships to ensure that generally, they all feel healthy for you.

Sometimes, comparison of relationships is necessary for quality assurance. This goes for all of your relationships, whether it be a friends-with-benefits arrangement or a long-term partnership. Different relationships thrive at different temperatures, but it is important that they are thriving.

What do you need to feel in all of your relationships, regardless of what titles they carry?

Your partners aren't supposed to use your insecurities as guiding principles for their choices in nonmonogamy. They can be sensitive to them, but they should not be governed by them.

We can be insecure about many things—financial status, intellect, body, even not having the same interests as our partners. It's OK to want your partners to be aware of and sensitive to your insecurities but not to the point that they restrict themselves or that you expect or demand that they restrict themselves because of your insecurities. That breeds resentment in your partners and that removes the opportunity for you to do your own self-work on your insecurities. It is not your partners' job to insulate your insecurities.

Have you ever had a partner who expected you to be governed by their insecurities? How did that make you feel?

Resist the urge to attempt to control the pace of your partners' relationships with others because you need time to process it. Instead, try finding the reason why the speed makes you uncomfortable and address that.

Maybe you didn't expect your partner to fall for their new person so quickly. Maybe you are feeling like you are less important to them now because they have such a strong connection with this new person. Maybe you are struggling to form your own connections and seeing your partner taking off in a new relationship bothers you. ❀ Whatever it is, it's better to deal with what is going on than to attempt to control a relationship you aren't in by asking them to cool down. ❀ It's OK to bring up your concerns about your partner moving too fast with a person, especially when you are worried they are making unwise choices in the relationship, but do so with the understanding that your partner still gets to decide for themselves how slow or fast they wish to move.

Have you ever had a partner ask you to slow down or have you asked a partner to slow down with someone else? If so, what was the outcome?

Don't be surprised if you introduced nonmonogamy in your relationship but your partner is the one who "takes off" and seems to have more "success." Resist the urge to want to pull back.

While I didn't introduce nonmonogamy into my marriage theoretically, I was definitely the catalyst for it and I just knew that I would be the one who had more "success" at it since my spouse was extremely introverted and recoiled from most social interactions. What happened, however, was the complete opposite of what I expected. My spouse had relative ease (my estimation) in forming relationships of substance and I struggled to do so. ❦ Just because a person introduces nonmonogamy to their partner, it doesn't mean that they'll have an easier time of it than their partner does. They might find the reverse happens and it is them who struggles while their partner flourishes. Often, the struggling partner may wish to dial back or make their partner slow down so they can catch up but I don't think that's fair, especially if they were the one initially pushing for it. ❦ Remember that success is subjective, nonmonogamy is an individual journey even when you are in a couple, and it's not a competition. This is all part of the dance. Tune in to your own music and sway to the rhythm that's playing for *you*.

Have you ever thought that a partner was more "successful" at polyamory than you were? If so, what led you to believe that?

Make sure you are asking for consent before tagging potential or existing partners in social media posts. Not everyone is "out" in all areas of their lives and some people are very private about their romantic lives.

I'm a huge fan of online public displays of affection and a self-proclaimed social media whore. I tag myself everywhere doing everything. I'm also very much out and have inadvertently "outed" people who are connected to me. This is also why I now only date people who are completely out and who don't mind being tagged and featured in social media posts with me. It makes things easier on everyone. ❧ Some people don't like online public displays of affection, aren't fully out (which is their choice) or like to keep their personal life private. Remember that someone not wanting to be on social media doesn't necessarily indicate that they are being shady in their relationships. Ask for consent before posting photos or information about others on your social media pages. This advice is good for all your relationships, whether with romantic partners, friends, family or others.

Do you ask for consent before posting about others on your social media pages? Do you care that people ask for consent before posting about you on their page?

Polyamory is like a dance. The music changes, the partners change, the steps change. The only constant is me. As long as I make sure that my footing is sure and solid, I know I'll be OK.

When I'm guiding people in polyamory, I remind them that "It's all part of the dance." The external factors of polyamory, I can't control. I can only control myself. So, when the partners change or the music changes or the steps change to this dance, I focus on making sure my footing is solid and I'm grounded within myself. I find that I enjoy the dance more when that is my focus.

What makes you feel sure in your footing in polyamory?

Observing our partners dating others can give us insight into their character in ways that can change our opinion of them, sometimes for the better and sometimes for the worse.

In monogamy, the only romantic relationship you observe your partner moving in is with you. In nonmonogamy, you not only observe how they move with you, but also how they move with others. Sometimes, what we see can endear us more to our partners. Other times, it can cause us to question their character in a negative way. ❀ I have noticed that my partners' dating choices, people choices and relationship choices can make me look at them in not-so-favorable ways.

What behaviors could your partner exhibit
in another relationship that would cause you
to change your opinion of them?

Day 187

It is not ethical to "bait and switch" potential partners by starting the connection as an individual and once desire is established, telling them that they must also be open to dating your other partner. Let people know this up front.

I can't tell you how many times I have heard stories of people excited about a new dating connection only to have their hopes dashed down the line as the person informs them that in order to continue in their relationship, they must be willing to date the new connection's partner(s). The person who thought they were building a relationship with an individual has to decide whether to lose a connection they enjoy or date people they weren't prepared to or aren't interested in dating. ❧ A person who does this might say, "Well, I need to be sure I like them first before I integrate them with my other partner(s)," but it is possible to do that while being transparent about your ultimate goal. You can say, "My partner(s) and I are seeking someone we all can date so I am connecting to you with the intent of you also dating them at some point."

Have you ever had someone "bait and switch" you in polyamory? How so?

Measure your success in polyamory not by the number of partners or relationships you have but by what poly is doing to you. Are you growing? Are you loving yourself and others more authentically? Are you learning more about yourself?

In 2019, I started the year off with five partners. By October, I was down to one. If my measure of being successful in nonmonogamy had been about how many partners I had or partnerships I was able to maintain, I would have felt like a failure. But I had grown emotionally, seen positive changes in my approach to nonmonogamy and my polyamorous life was peaceful even with the breakups. ❀ I make my measure of success in polyamory about what it's doing to me. That way, no matter what happens in my relationships, I know it's "working" because it's helping me become a better person.

How has polyamory helped you to grow as a person?

Sometimes, when I have felt dislike toward my metamours, it wasn't about them but what I felt about myself in comparison to them. If they activate my insecurities, it's easier to dislike them than it is to dislike myself.

Let me start this by saying that it's OK to have metamours you don't mesh well with or who just aren't people you enjoy or connect with. I have had metamours I didn't like for no other reason than we just didn't click. However, I have also had times where I had to examine my dislike of a metamour or a potential metamour because I realized that my dislike of them had nothing to do with them on a personal level and everything to do with how my partner's estimation of them made me feel about myself. ❧ If I thought the person was more attractive than me, more interesting, better suited for my partner, had more in common with them, or whatever it was, it was easier to turn that into dislike of them instead of dislike of me for not being them. ❧ If you notice an impulse to dislike people your partner is seeing before you even get a decent chance to get a feel for them, examine that. It might be more about you than them.

Have you found yourself disliking a metamour because you felt insecure about yourself in comparison? What insecurities caused your dislike?

Hold firm boundaries around your quality time with your partners, especially when it comes to processing emotions with one partner about spending time with another.

Imagine that you have a date night scheduled to see a movie with one of your partners. You mention the movie you're seeing to your other partner and they get upset because they wanted to see that movie with you first. It begins an emotional discussion between the two of you. While you are on your date, instead of being present with your partner, you're texting your other partner to discuss their feelings about you seeing the movie with someone else. Now the partner you're with is upset because you spent the entire date on your phone texting your other partner. ❀ Our partners deserve us being present when we set aside time for them and it is OK to tell your other partner that you are on a date and will pick the discussion back up when you are free. Hold firm boundaries with your partners about the importance of your time with other partners.

Are you intentional about being present during your time with a partner, even when you are in conflict with another partner? How do you hold your boundaries around time with your partners?

Be prepared to feel a lot of emotions in nonmonogamy, often directly opposed emotions simultaneously. Learn to hold space for all of them.

Welcome to the land of the feels. One of the interesting things about nonmonogamy is that you can find yourself feeling two completely opposite emotions at the same time. You can be happy that your partner is enjoying their relationship with another and sad that you are struggling to find a partner. You can feel extremely fulfilled in one relationship and devastated about a breakup in another relationship. Learn to hold space for them all. There is no right way to feel. Your feelings are just your feelings. Meet them all with compassion and love.

What opposing emotions have you experienced simultaneously while navigating polyamory?

Our metamours' challenges can produce feelings of guilt for us. If you know you did nothing particularly wrong, alleviate yourself of feeling guilty and simply have compassion. Remember that challenges are how people grow.

I believe it is wisest to navigate nonmonogamy in a way that allows both our partners and metamours to feel cared for and considered by us. There are times, however, when even with the most careful of movements, a metamour can experience challenging emotions about our relationship with our shared partner. When this happens, it is not uncommon to feel guilty that our metamour is struggling and believe ourselves to have caused them pain. ❀ If we know we didn't do anything wrong, willfully inappropriate or intentionally hurtful, then any guilt is not founded. Polyamory is challenging. Difficult emotions are unavoidable. Our metamours are human and we can be compassionate to their humanity without feeling guilty. And challenges in polyamory are how we grow—no one is exempt to that. ❀ If we don't manage our guilt, it may cause us to unnecessarily limit our relationship with our partner, resent our metamours, or place the burden of our guilt onto our metamours, none of which are healthy ways to deal with it. ❀ It's also OK to create boundaries around how much exposure you have to the challenges your metamours experience. You have a right to limit how much their challenges are shared with you.

Do you feel guilty about your metamours' struggles? If so, why?

When making agreements with your partners, remember that a situation may arise that does not fit neatly into what your agreement covers. It's hard to know the protocol in a situation that no one could have predicted and planned for.

Imagine that you and your nesting partner have an agreement that you won't take calls from other partners after 11 pm but one of your partners just received news that a family member was injured badly at 12 am and they want to call you for support. ❧ Or consider that you and your partner have an agreement that neither of you will spend the night at another person's house unless they are an established partner. Your partner goes on a date with a new person they are seeing and goes back to their house for a nightcap and gets food poisoning. They are too sick to drive and have to spend the night. ❧ We make agreements for what we presently believe we want and for situations that we expect based on what we foresee occurring. Even with the most careful consideration, it's not possible to account for every possibility and sometimes a situation will arise that no one could have predicted and that the standard agreements and guidelines don't really apply for. ❧ Remember the need for some flexibility when making agreements and the need to have grace and understanding when you or your partners find yourselves in situations that don't fit neatly between the lines.

What does being flexible about your relationship agreements mean to you and your partner(s)?

Day 194

When examining your relationship needs from a particular partner, make sure you are also being aware of whether those needs are reasonable for that partner to provide.

It's totally OK to have romantic needs, but sometimes the romantic expectations we have of a particular person aren't reasonable for them to provide. ❦ For example, it's OK to want to spend four days a week with a romantic partner but it's probably not reasonable to expect that a married person with children will be able to provide that for you. It's OK to want a romantic partner who wants to spend time at your house with you and your spouse and your kids for most of your time together, but it's probably not reasonable to expect a solo-polyamorous person who intentionally doesn't want kids and prefers parallel-poly to give you that. ❦ You can want what you want, but you don't always get to have whomever you want provide it for you.

What relationship expectations of you do you feel are reasonable? What relationship expectations of you would you feel are unreasonable?

We all need to unpack the notions that come with couple privilege, whether we are married, coupled, single or solo. The centering of couples is deeply ingrained in how we are socialized to view relationships.

Couple privilege is defined as the mainstream acceptance, validation, support, prioritization and centering of dyadic, coupled romantic relationships. It asserts that a "primary" coupled romantic relationship is the most important relationship structure and therefore most deserving of consideration, preservation, support and validation. It is deeply woven into the fabric of our society. ❀ When we enter nonmonogamy, we bring many beliefs and ideologies that we have received from the dominant social relationship culture, and couple privilege is one of them. When unchecked and unpacked, this can have harmful effects in nonmonogamy, with the greatest detrimental impact on people who are single, solo or relationship anarchists and other folks in relationships with people in coupled pairings. As with all forms of privilege, there are blatant and insidious ways that it exists within and interacts with all of us, whether we are the beneficiary of the privilege or the victim of it. ❀ It is important that we all confront and address couple privilege within ourselves and within our relationships, with the largest responsibility falling on those in coupled dynamics. None of us exist in a vacuum and we have all been shaped in some way by these beliefs. The de-centering of the couple as "king" is imperative to the wellness of nonmonogamous people.

Where does couple privilege exist in your beliefs? How have you had to unpack it?

Having a strong sense of self-worth in polyamory is important. Having self-worth means knowing that you deserve to be treated well.

In the beginning of my nonmonogamous journey, I struggled to establish relationships and often accepted treatment that was less than what I wanted because I felt like dating as a married woman meant I kinda had to take what I could get. Now that I'm further along, I have decided I will no longer allow people to tell me how they think I am worthy of being treated. I will decide how I am worthy of being treated and align myself with people who agree with that. ❀ I deserve to have joy in my relationships. I deserve to feel matched enthusiasm in my relationships. I deserve to feel cared for and appreciated even in times of conflict in my relationships. I deserve partners who demonstrate that they are just as concerned about pouring into me as they are about me pouring into them. Holding out for that is a gift I give to myself because I am worth it.

What do you believe you are worthy of in your relationships with others? Do the relationships you are in match that?

It's OK to want monogamy, but it's not OK to demand monogamy from whomever you want it with. It's OK to want polyamory, but it's not OK to demand polyamory from whomever you want it with.

Whether you started your relationship monogamously or nonmonogamously, remember that folks can change their minds. Sometimes, you will reach an impasse and go your separate ways. But demanding that a person give you a relationship style that they don't want isn't the right move. It is not their job to give that to you.

Have you ever had a partner demand monogamy or nonmonogamy from you? If so, how did that work out?

Day 198

Our partners deserve privacy in their relationships with others and so do our metamours. Privacy is not the same as hiding information. Learn to respect that you don't need to know some things.

I once had a partner who was more private than I was. Early on in my polyamory journey, I felt I needed a lot of information about their relationships with others to feel secure. I would go through my partner's phone, read things that weren't meant for me and be far too intrusive with my questioning. Eventually, my partner had to put their foot down. It was difficult to deal with at the time, but I'm ultimately grateful that they did so. I needed to learn to respect their right to privacy in their relationships with others and to also respect the privacy of my metamours. I'm not entitled to every little detail I want about their relationships. I also had to learn to live on less information. ❋ Your partners and their partners deserve you respecting their privacy. You are also allowed, and should stand up for, your sense of privacy in all of your relationships. Privacy is not secrecy and transparency is different from unlimited access to all information.

What needs for privacy do you have in your relationships?

Do away with the use of words like "dirty" and "clean" to talk about STI status. These words perpetuate stigmas and make safe disclosure harder.

Hello, my name is Evita and I have HSV-2. I was diagnosed in 2016. I don't know who I contracted it from. I practiced safer sex for the most part. Currently, I manage my HSV-2 with a daily medication and supplement and by general care for my physical health. To the best of my ability, I inform people before I have sex with them that I am positive (I have had instances where that didn't happen but I informed them immediately afterward). To my knowledge, none of my partners has contracted the virus from me. There are still people who want to have sex with me knowing this information. I am not ashamed of myself for it. ❀ I am not dirty. I am not unworthy of a healthy sex life because of it. I am a human with a medical condition. And I'm passionate about erasing the stigmas people with STIs face by being open about my own. STI stigma has a lot to do with sex negativity and shame. If we keep upholding it, we make it hard for people to have healthy, open, honest and transparent conversations about sexual health and STI status. ❀ If you have an STI, you are not dirty and you are also worthy of sex, love and pleasure exactly as you are.

How do you encourage honest, shame-free conversations about STI status among your partners?

You can be poly in the projects, poly on food stamps, poly in Section 8 housing. Polyamory is a relationship orientation that shouldn't be restricted to certain classes of people.

I am weary of seeing conversations around whether or not polyamory is for "lower-class" persons. You can date cheaply. Not everyone is trying to have multiple spouses and large households full of partners. Does having more access to financial resources make living polyamorously easier? Sure. But having more access to financial resources makes life easier in general, not just polyamory. ❀ We need to understand that capitalism and classism dictate that only affluent people are worthy of pleasure and that people of lower economic classes should be focusing all of their energy and time on trying to change their economic status. It's garbage. You don't have to be rich to be poly and you are worthy of the love you want regardless of what you have in the bank. Believe that.

How have you have experienced classism in polyamory?

Your emotions reveal the truth about how you feel but they don't always reflect reality, and they definitely can't tell you the truth about your partners' thoughts, feelings or motivations.

I try to remember this when I recognize that my feelings are telling me a story about reality, especially when they are telling me a story about my partners and what I think is going on with them. I remind myself that when I am upset about something my partners have done, it's more than likely because I think their motivations are what my motivation would have been had I done that thing. But they are different people with different thoughts and motivations than I have. ❧ I'm not saying that we shouldn't listen to our feelings—they are valid and they have valuable information for us—but they don't tell us the whole truth, just the truth about how we feel. They definitely can't tell us what is true for others.

Do you find it difficult to separate your emotional narratives from reality? What tools have you developed to work on this?

Your partners can't make you feel secure. They can only do their best to reassure you that they care. You also can't make your partners feel secure, but can do your best to reassure them that you care.

If you struggle with feeling secure in relationships, non-monogamy will definitely challenge that. Our partners can only do so much to reassure us of their regard for us. If you find yourself struggling to feel secure in your partnerships, and you can honestly say that your partners do a good job of loving you, then you need to do some internal work to become a more secure person. ❦ It's also good to remember that you can't make a person feel secure. If you're doing the best you can to show someone you care and it doesn't ever seem to be enough, more than likely, that person needs to either work on being a more secure person in their relationship to you or admit that they need more than what you can give them and deal with that. ❦ I'm not talking about relationships where you aren't being treated well or where there have been clear violations of trust or lack of regard. Pretty much nobody would feel secure in a relationship where that's what's happening.

How do you work on feeling secure in your relationships? How do your partners show up for you to help with that work?

Just like romantic relationships look much different in nonmonogamy than in monogamy, breakups look different too. As you are considering how you want your relationships to work, also consider how you'd like them to end.

Breaking up is hard to do. And it becomes even more complicated in nonmonogamy. Our communities are often small. More than likely, you'll be interacting with your exes or your partner's exes. The reasons for ending relationships can be different in nonmonogamy. Oftentimes, they have to do with circumstances and not lack of desire to be with a person. Also, relationship transitions are more common in nonmonogamy since the relationship "scripts" often don't apply, so it's easier to shift to a different space with a person and maintain the connection while not holding tightly to it being a certain way. ❀ When to end a relationship is a personal choice and it helps to consider and discuss with your partners how you want to exit the relationship as much as how you want to enter it.

What are some of your desires and needs during a breakup?

If your launch into nonmonogamy was infidelity, it's going to be much harder to move forward in your relationship with your partner. Polyamory is a huge trust exercise and you started in broken trust.

I see this so much that I have a metaphor for it. It's like lining up at a start line with your partner to run a race together and then shooting them in the foot before the race starts. You've injured them and they now have to start the journey nursing a deep wound. I'm not saying that this situation never works out, but you must acknowledge the harm you caused by being unfaithful and recognize that you have made this harder for your partner to work through. Just becoming nonmonogamous isn't going to heal the damage you caused. ❧ And this isn't just reserved to having sex with another person when you were monogamous. If you participated in any activity that was a breach of the contract of monogamy you had with a person, whether emotional or physical, that counts. If you're in a monogamous relationship and questioning whether or not you want to be nonmonogamous, have the conversation before you "cheat."

Has a partner ever cheated on you and then presented nonmonogamy to you? If so, did that impact your ability to trust them?

While your intent may be to show consideration, asking a partner if they are comfortable with something and making their comfort the deciding factor for your decision places the burden of your choice in their lap.

It's a good thing to consider your partners' comfort when you are weighing your decisions in polyamory and to let them know their comfort is important to you, but making their comfort the deciding factor for the choices you make is tricky. It places the weight of your choices on them. If they aren't comfortable and they are honest, it can feel like they are controlling or limiting you and that can result in them not being honest about their genuine feelings to avoid that. It can also result in feeling like you have to ask your partners for permission to do the things that you want, which can lead to resentment. ✾ To me, the better way to navigate this is by establishing with your partner what behaviors are permissible and making your choices within those boundaries. That way, you can come to them with your choices already decided and hold space for whatever discomfort they have without their discomfort dictating your decisions. And if you have a desire outside of the established guidelines, communicate that to your partner and ask what kind of support they think they may need to be more at ease with your decisions.

Have you ever had a partner make your comfort the deciding factor for something they wanted to do in polyamory? If so, how did that make you feel?

There's learning you can have multiple relationships and then there's learning how to have multiple relationships *well*, and that is a process.

Just because you can have ten relationships, doesn't mean you have the resources, tools, know-how or capacity to have ten functioning relationships. When entering nonmonogamy, the prospect of being able to have as many partners as you want is exciting, but it takes time to learn how to have multiple partnerships *well*. Don't bite off much more than you can chew. Pace yourself.

What does having multiple relationships well mean to you?

When communicating discomfort in polyamory, discuss what you're feeling without placing responsibility for your feelings on your partner.

When I first started my nonmonogamous journey, I had to develop this skill. Many of my initial discussions with my partner about my discomforts went sideways because what I said and the way I phrased things came off as accusatory and they became defensive. There's a difference between saying, "You're doing this thing that makes me uncomfortable" and saying, "You're doing this thing and I'm feeling discomfort about it." It's an important distinction. Your partner will hear you better when they don't feel like they're warding off blows to connect to your message.

What can partners say to you that cause you to feel as if they are making you responsible for their emotions?

Polyamory is like exercise in that you want to set goals and challenge yourself to grow, but you have to be mindful of where you are currently and not push yourself to the point of injury trying to be "better" at it.

You might want to be in the place where you can spend the whole weekend in a cabin with your love and their other love and all get along well and enjoy it, but you might not be at that place yet and that's OK. I have seen so many people push themselves into interactions with their partners and metamours, trying to be "better" than where they are, and then have those attempts implode horribly and cause damage to everyone involved. Yes, it's good to challenge ourselves because that's how we grow. But don't push yourself too far and don't judge yourself for where you are. If you keep your goals in mind and work toward them, you'll get there. ❧ It's also important to note that where we are in our journey isn't grounds for dictating what our partners do. For example, you may find your partner spending the entire weekend with another love really hard, but that doesn't mean that your partner should cancel their weekend. Rather, you should be aware it will be a challenge for you and think critically about ways you can support yourself and ways your partner can aid you in that process while also maintaining their autonomy.

Have you ever pushed yourself too far in polyamory? How did that turn out?

No matter who it is, it's not OK for someone to be dismissive, invasive, inconsiderate or disrespectful about the fact that you're nonmonogamous. You have the right to create boundaries between yourself and someone who is behaving that way towards you.

It doesn't matter if it's a partner, a friend, a family member, a coworker, anyone. While someone may struggle to understand or even support you being nonmonogamous, that does not give them the right to disrespect you, disregard you or make you uncomfortable because of it. When someone in your life is demonstrating that they cannot honor your nonmonogamy because of their personal opinions or biases about it, it is your right and duty to yourself to create boundaries with that person for your own safety, or perhaps even to remove them from your life. ❀ Just because polyamory isn't the norm, doesn't mean it is less worthy of respect. Stand up for yourself and your authentic truth.

Have you ever had to remove someone from your life for being disrespectful or invalidating to your nonmonogamy? Is there someone in your life you need to reevaluate your relationship with because of this?

Day 210

Many couples begin nonmonogamy with an edict that they don't fall in love with anyone else or don't fall "too deeply." You can't dictate what someone else does with their feelings, only what you do with your own.

This has tripped up many a couple in nonmonogamy. They agree that they won't develop feelings for anyone else or that they won't develop "deep" feelings for anyone else and then when someone does, the other feels betrayed and upset. Feelings are hard enough to control within oneself, and it's even harder to try to control what other people do with theirs. You also can't always make agreements for your future self. You don't know who you're going to meet or how you're going to feel about someone down the line. It's better to just concern yourself with what you wish to do with your own feelings and respect your partner's right to do the same.

Have you ever sought to control the feelings of your partners or had a partner try to control your feelings? If so, what was the outcome?

Polyamory can bring up a lot of the trauma we have experienced around love. We must remember that our partners can't heal our trauma for us and we can't heal their trauma for them.

I have a son who was diagnosed with brain cancer at six years old. As his mother, if I could have taken his tumor into my body and fought it for him, I would have because I love him. The reality, however, is that I couldn't heal for him. Even if I was an oncologist, I would have only been able to facilitate to the best of my ability the circumstances for him to heal, but at some point his body would have to take over and do its own work to heal. ❦ Similarly, my partners cannot heal my hurts around love, worthiness, insecurity or feeling desirable. They can care and support me as I heal but they can't heal me and I can't heal them. Our healing is our own work. When I am feeling triggered by something a partner is doing, it is not their job to figure out what is bothering me, what hurt or trauma is being activated and what I need to soothe the pain. That work is mine. And they also have a responsibility to do that work for themselves.

How do you take on the responsibility of trying to heal your partners?

Monogamy is a zero-sum game and thus creates a scarcity mindset around romantic love. It helps to shift the narrative from scarcity to abundance as we seek to connect with others.

A "zero-sum game" is one where a player's gain is another player's loss. In monogamy, if someone gets the person you want, you don't get that person. This causes us to view romantic love as something we must compete for and cling to. There's a limited number of people in the world and many other people vying for them. ❦ Then we enter polyamory, and the world opens up. Or does it? We often carry the same limiting beliefs into our nonmonogamous practice. We can feel fear as our partners connect to others. We can hold on to relationships that don't serve us because finding other people to connect with is hard so we settle for less than we are worth. We can refuse to let go of partners who want to move on because we aren't sure we'll find someone else. ❦ Shifting our mindset from seeing the world as a place of love scarcity to a place of love abundance is hard work, especially if you have lived through trauma or marginalization, or if you lacked a foundation of love in your life. But it is necessary work. When we don't see the world as a place where love must be grappled for, we are much more secure in our relationships with others. ❦ Monogamous people can also benefit from doing this work. Letting go of scarcity in love can revolutionize your relationships.

Do you feel scarcity around love? If so, what do you think that scarcity stems from?

When things don't work out with someone or we get rejected, it can be a huge disappointment. I try to see those experiences as the universe knowing that a person isn't right for me, even if I don't see it.

"Learn to trust the judgment of the universe when it closes a door." This is a personal saying I created for myself after a huge dating disappointment I experienced early on in my journey. I was devastated that something didn't work out and it wasn't until a year or so later that I found out they were not a good person to be with. ✻ It's normal to be disappointed when things don't work out with someone you are really into but sometimes, that turns out to be a huge blessing. Feel your valid feelings and then trust that the right folks are in the stars for you.

What is a blessing you received from the ending of your last relationship?

Polyamory can trigger our beliefs around our attractiveness. It's easy to wonder why we aren't as popular as some other folks or why we have a harder time garnering interest than others. It's OK to feel that.

I have spent my entire life being the "ugly" friend—the one who hardly got asked out. I have struggled to find people who were interested in me. When I became nonmonogamous, interacting in polyamorous spaces triggered all those old wounds. Being in groups where you can see who gets more attention and who doesn't can transport us right back to being the awkward teen in high school wondering why no one wants to go to prom with us. ❀ When this triggers my negative self-talk about not being the "pretty girl" and when I'm feeling down about not having the experience I want or all the suitors to choose from, I remember that everyone has an audience. Some people's audience can pack out a big stadium. They have thousands of fans. For some people, their audience can only fill a local coffee shop but those faithful fans will be at every show. Instead of lamenting about the fans I don't have, I'm going to celebrate the ones I do have.

Have you ever felt insecure about not being "popular" in your polyamorous community? What was happening that made you feel this way?

It's OK to be disappointed when someone you were interested in just wants to be friends. It's also OK to decline their offer of friendship if that's not what you want from them. Being upset with them about their choice isn't OK.

It's normal to be disappointed that the kind of relationship experience you wanted with a person isn't going to happen. It's also OK to not accept their offer of friendship if you are unable to. That's not wrong. But acting like they owed you what you wanted from them and being upset at them or hanging around pretending to accept friendship when you're really just continuing to hope they'll change their mind isn't the right move. ❧ Remember that what you ultimately want is someone who wants you in the way you want them. Lose the belief that basic human decency should grant you access to whatever you want from a person. Learn to be direct about your desires with folks so you can both make choices sooner about how you want to connect. No one owes us any kind of interaction and we also don't owe anyone anything other than what we want. It doesn't make them a bad person and it doesn't make you a bad person.

How do you react to someone only wanting to be friends with you when you are romantically interested in them? Has someone ever had a negative reaction to you wanting to be friends when they were romantically interested in you?

Sometimes when I'm struggling with jealousy, I substitute whatever my partner is doing to thinking of them as being with a friend. It helps to shift my feelings and provides perspective.

I figured this out while thinking about picking up my former husband's socks. If I was at home while he was out with a friend and I noticed he left a sock on the floor, I might grumble to myself about it, but I'd pick up the sock with little emotional agitation. If he was on a date, however, I would be much more bothered about it and get upset that he was on a date while I was "picking up after him" (something I didn't *have* to do). I began to question the difference in response. Whether he was out on a date or with a friend, it was essentially the same thing—he was using his time to fulfill himself with a person he wished to interact with. ❧ I began to experiment with what else I could substitute by saying, "Would I feel this way if he was out with a friend?" Most of the time, the answer was no. A friend, like a partner, is an important person in someone's life. Reframing my thinking helped me to feel less jealous because I wasn't viewing my partner's romantic time with others as a special circumstance. They just became instances where my partner was spending time with people who were special to them. This didn't completely eradicate the jealousy, but it did reduce it.

Do you notice a difference in the discomfort you feel when your partner is with another partner versus when they are with a friend? If so, why does it feel different for you?

What jealousy or insecurity means for someone else won't be the same as what it means for you. Avoid judging people for having normal human emotions.

When I first began this journey, I joined a lot of online groups and noticed that very few people were talking about their struggles in nonmonogamy. There were many posts about feeling compersion and joy and I was confused because that wasn't my experience. ❧ Then I made a post about having some difficult feelings and saw why people weren't sharing their downs as much. I was attacked so viciously on that post that I cried. Posting about jealousy resulted in me being called everything from immature to controlling to possessive to unenlightened. Admitting to insecurity led to people being told they were petty and competitive and needed to work on their confidence. I couldn't understand why people were so opposed to others expressing what felt like normal human emotions to me. ❧ It's fine for you to decide what an emotion is for you, but stop judging people for having their genuine emotions. It may mean something different for them. And it's hard enough to seek support for an emotion without judging yourself for feeling it, let alone knowing you're going to face judgment from others for expressing it. Let's start creating safe spaces for people to be real about their feelings. I'm not saying to allow unhealthy behavior to go unchallenged, but just to allow folks to feel their feelings.

What does it mean to you when you are feeling jealous or insecure? Do you project that same meaning onto your partners when they are feeling jealous or insecure?

Figuring out what you need to combat your own jealousies or insecurities is personal work. What works for someone else may not work for you.

The tools that I present here to handle difficult emotions are ones that I developed along my personal journey. Many times, people will ask me things like, "What if this doesn't work and I'm still feeling jealous?" or say, "I tried this and it still didn't help." My response is always, "OK." What has worked for me may not work for you. The tools I've created for myself may not speak to your emotions like they speak to mine. And sometimes, my tools don't even work for me and I find myself in situations where I'm having to create new ones. ❧ Yes, it's good to have outlets where you can learn tools that you might find helpful but that isn't going to replace you doing your own work to get to know your jealousies and insecurities intimately so you know exactly what you need and exactly how to minister to them. Sometimes, other people's tools will be useful but sometimes, you will have to create your own. Having a personalized jealousy plan is the optimal setup for success.

What personal tools have you developed to navigate your own jealousies or insecurities?

It is normal for polyamory to be challenging, especially in the beginning of your journey, but at some point, there should be an improvement in how you navigate it. If that's not the case, examine why.

Polyamory ain't for the faint of heart. I struggled considerably in my early journey on this path and still do. I'm not afraid to admit that. At some point, though, with enough time, practice and personal work, it became easier. I developed tools to self-soothe and learned how to advocate for my needs, speak up about my boundaries, be compassionate and empathetic to my partners, recognize their autonomy more readily, own up to my mistakes and accept the work of unpacking monogamy. I'm not perfect by any stretch, and I know I will never "arrive," but the path got more sure, more peaceful and lighter along the way. ❀ If you find that you have been at this a while and you are still deeply struggling along your walk, examine the why. Maybe it's that your current partner or partners are the wrong people to navigate it with, maybe your partner choices need reevaluating, maybe you've been avoiding some deeper work, maybe you're just monogamous. Whatever the answer, be brave enough to find out what it is. ❀ While I know that there will always be challenges along this path, it shouldn't be one of perpetual sadness and pain. You deserve to have joy in your polyamory.

In what ways has polyamory gotten easier for you? In what ways is it still challenging?

If you wrestle with feeling guilty when your partners are struggling emotionally in polyamory, remember that holding on to your autonomy can be uncomfortable for those you love but you aren't wrong for it.

Our guilt can make listening and holding space for our partner's struggles challenging. It's hard to watch a person you care about be in pain about something and even harder if that pain is connected to something you are doing. ❧ You are not wrong for holding on to your autonomy, though, and if you didn't violate an agreement with your partner, then while they may not like what you did, logically, you weren't wrong for doing it. So your feelings of guilt are what you have to examine and let go of. You can feel sad that they are experiencing pain and validate that while also maintaining that you aren't responsible for it. ❧ You aren't trying to hurt your partner—you're trying to live your life doing what you feel is best for you and sometimes, your partners may feel discomfort about those choices.

Do you struggle with feeling guilty when your partners experience discomfort around your choices? If so, what are some things you can say to yourself to help you hold firm to your decisions?

You deserve to give yourself the same compassion and empathy you extend to your partners. If you don't judge them for their struggles in nonmonogamy, don't judge yourself for yours.

I often find that people show up to their partners' emotions in nonmonogamy with far more compassion and empathy than they extend to their own emotions. ❧ Have you ever had a conversation with your partner about some emotions they struggled to tell you about and when they finally felt safe enough to express them, you just wrapped their feelings in love and compassion? Do you treat yourself with the same ready love and compassion when you are having difficult emotions? ❧ We can be most harsh with ourselves. We can understand and empathize with the feelings of others and in the same breath berate ourselves for the same feelings. Don't do that to yourself. Your feelings deserve love and compassion, most of all from you.

How do you find self-compassion hard?

Don't run from challenges in polyamory—that's how we grow. With each challenge you navigate, you get stronger, wiser and more sure of yourself and your wants and needs. They are necessary.

While challenges aren't fun, they have benefits. When we face a challenging situation or emotion in nonmonogamy and we get through it, we gain many things: wisdom, insight, fortitude, empowerment, confidence. All of the emotions or insecurities that we are so terrified of dealing with lose their strength. They become less acute and we become more self-assured in our ability to handle them. None of this can happen without challenges.

How can you change your perception of challenges and embrace them when they occur?

If you decide to let the feelings of your partners determine your choices, it is unfair to blame them for that decision. Own that at the time, what was more important to you was choosing their comfort over your desires.

If you choose to allow your partners' emotions to determine what you do in polyamory, own that choice. The comfort of your partners has more value to you. It is normal to be bothered by feeling limited by their emotions, but it is unfair to blame and resent them for choices you made, especially if they didn't ask you to prioritize their emotions over your genuine desires to begin with. ❧ If your partner has so many difficult emotions that you struggle to feel free to make your authentic choices, reevaluate if that person and the relationship you have with them is right for you. Also reevaluate if you struggle to hold room for your own autonomy while making space for your partners to have their genuine emotions about that because you may have some guilt around being nonmonogamous or difficulties with being a people-pleaser. ❧ This advice doesn't refer to circumstances where your partner having difficult emotions has a directly harmful impact on you, like in an abusive situation or a relationship that has an uneven power dynamic at play. Sometimes, this choice is made for self-preservation and that is valid. Still, own that necessity and begin to address the more pressing concern that you may need to exit or change that relationship.

In what ways do you choose the comfort of your partners over your desires? Do you internally resent your partners for that?

It's important to have partners who enthusiastically reassure us but it's just as important that we ask for reassurance. Our partners aren't mind readers.

Yes, it's important to have partners who enthusiastically offer reassurance when we need it, but we have a responsibility to ask for it and not expect our partners to be mind readers. And be specific. If it's your desirability that you're struggling with, ask to be reminded that your partner is still attracted to you. Struggling to believe they still enjoy your company? Ask to be reminded that they still have fun with you. It'll be much more helpful when your partners know which specific insecurity you want them to speak to. ❧ Keep in mind that sometimes we can need too much reassurance and that can be draining on our partners. If you find yourself needing constant reassurance from a partner, examine why you are struggling so hard to feel secure.

How is asking for reassurance difficult for you?

When someone breaks up with us, it can become difficult not to become overly critical of ourselves, assessing all the ways we "failed." Extend yourself grace.

"Where did I go wrong?" "Why wasn't I enough?" "What could I have done more to make this person stay?" These are all questions that we grapple with when someone we care about ends or changes their relationship with us. It is healthy to assess what happened in a relationship that is ending and to go over how we contributed to the outcome, but we don't need to be hard on ourselves and add unnecessary suffering to what is likely an already painful situation. You're already grieving the loss. Beating yourself up about it will only prolong the time it will take you to heal. ❀ If you did the best that you could, then there was nothing more you could do. Make peace with that. If you could have done better, own that, learn and move forward with that new knowledge. In all of this, offer yourself grace. It's the most loving thing you can do to care for yourself.

How are you hard on yourself when a relationship ends?

When I make my polyamorous journey about my relationships with others, I often find hurt, dissatisfaction and disappointment. When I make it about myself, I find peace.

Shifting my measure of my personal "success" in polyamory from how many partners I have or how many relationships I'm in or how many people I'm connecting with to how I'm growing, unlearning old patterns and maturing as a person as a result of my practice has been affirming for me. Partners have come and gone but what has remained steady and constant is my commitment to continue to progress, heal and work toward becoming the person I desire to be in my relationships with my loved ones. ❦ When I measured my success by how many people I was with, it felt fickle. My self-esteem in polyamory had extreme highs and lows based on what was happening in relationship to the other people I had in my life. Learning to measure my success on my own growth and understanding felt more solid and has given me more confidence. It means I am affirming myself and not relying on what was going on with others to be my most important source of validation.

How do you measure your success in polyamory in ways that have nothing to do with others?

If you started your polyamorous journey from a background of cheating, you will likely struggle with the transparency of polyamory because you are used to conducting your nonmonogamy in a shroud of secrecy.

I see this often, especially in couples where one person cheated because they weren't aware that they could choose to be nonmonogamous ethically. It's not having multiple relationships that they struggle with, it's being honest about it. When you are used to seeing your nonmonogamy as something you have to hide, it can be hard to bring it into the light. ❋ Work on whatever shame you have about it or disbelief that someone can love you in your nonmonogamous existence. You won't be able to build trust if you are still acting like you have to hide yourself.

What about the transparency of polyamory feels uncomfortable for you?

After a breakup, the prospect of love can feel bleak. But it stands to reason that if you found love before, you can find love again. Keep hope alive.

When a door "closes" on love, it can feel like you'll never find another open one. It's OK to feel that way but try to remember that love is all around us and within us, too. Believe in the possibility of new love, love that is more suited to who you are now, love that can restore your faith in its blessings for you.

When you experience a breakup or disappointment in love, what can you do to return to feeling hopeful about love again?

It is one thing to want to have a "primary" relationship with someone and to make someone your primary partner. It is another thing to expect that person to also make you primary to them.

It's fine if you organize your relationships in a way that designates one (or more) of your partners as "primary," but you need to be clear on whether you also have the expectation that your partner or partners will also make you primary, because that needs to be communicated and agreed upon. ❀ You can make a partner primary without the expectation that they make you primary or you can choose partners who also want primary relationships so that you are on the same page with one another. But making someone primary and expecting them to do the same for you without expressly stating that to them and agreeing to those terms sets you both up for frustration and misunderstanding.

Do you desire to have a primary partner? Do you desire to be primary to your partner? What does being primary mean to you?

When a partner asks us to agree to something we don't want or asks us for a consideration we are not able or willing to provide, it can feel unkind to say no. However, it is possible to say no compassionately.

Our partners can sometimes ask us for accommodations or to make agreements that we can't or don't want to provide, things that may limit our relationships with others or control how we navigate polyamory. Saying no to these requests can be hard as it may feel unkind to disappoint them and not give them what they want because we care about them. ❧ What is actually unkind is making agreements that we know we don't want (which is essentially being dishonest), saying yes and then harboring resentment, or agreeing to things we can't or don't want, only to fail at keeping our word. It is possible to say no with care. ❧ It's saying, "I am unwilling or incapable of granting this request but I do care about your needs. Is there something similar we can come up with that will provide what you want and is something I am willing and able to give?"

What about saying no to your partners feels most uncomfortable to you?

Don't try to manage your partners' emotions by telling them what you think they want you to say if that's not in alignment with what you actually want.

Consider this example: Shane and Pat are in a relationship. Pat begins dating an exciting new person and Shane is struggling with it. Pat has a date with the new person on Friday and tells Shane that nothing physical will happen because they want to take things slowly. That's not really what Pat wants, though. Pat is simply saying this because they think it's what Shane wants to hear or what Shane wants Pat to want. ❀ Friday comes and Pat goes on the date and ends up getting physical with their new boo. When they tell Shane, Shane is understandably upset. Shane feels they can't trust Pat and that Pat went against their word by doing something they said they didn't want to do. What actually happened, however, was that Pat was trying to manage Shane's emotions by saying what they thought Shane wanted to hear, even though Pat really wanted something else. ❀ Moral of the story: Communicate what you genuinely want, not what you think your partner wants you to want. Your true desires always come out and it's better for everyone if you're honest about them. Also, denying yourself something that your partner isn't asking you to do can lead to you feeling frustrated at them for it.

Do you tell your partners what you think they want to hear instead of what your genuine desires are? If so, why?

When you are assessing your boundaries in nonmonogamy, make sure to check in with yourself to assess if they are actually your boundaries or measures you are using to punish your partners.

I will never advocate for challenging someone's boundaries. When someone institutes a boundary with you, your immediate action should be compliance. What I'm saying is to check in with yourself to make sure your boundaries are coming from a genuine place and not from a desire to stick it to your partners for doing things in polyamory that make you uncomfortable or you don't like. ❧ For example, Cam and Trace are nested partners. Trace has a new partner and has decided to begin a sexual relationship with them. Cam is uncomfortable about this and tells Trace that their boundary is that they will sleep in the guest room for three days whenever Trace comes back from a date with their new partner. If Cam were being honest with themselves, their boundary isn't about what they need but about punishing Trace for having a new sexual partner. Is Cam wrong for instituting that boundary? No. But is this the best way to deal with their discomfort? Also no. And it hurts Trace because it causes them to have to weigh an uncomfortable choice every time they interact with their new partner. ❧ It's often not obvious how we hurt others when we are hurting, so examine your motivations. I'm not saying negotiate your boundaries with others, but to negotiate them within yourself.

Have you ever created a boundary that was actually a punitive measure for your partners? If so, what helped you to recognize that you were trying to punish them?

While it is important to remember that our partners aren't mind readers and to ask for what we need and want from them, it is also true that there are some things we don't want to have to ask for.

This is something I have personally struggled with. I absolutely believe that we need to ask for what we need and want in relationships, but I found that I was asking for things from people that I didn't feel like I should have to ask for. I realized that I wanted to be in relationships with people who already showed up to loving me in ways I could readily perceive because that was the kind of person they were and how they naturally showed up to love. ❀ So now, my focus is on continuing to ask for my needs and wants while also making sure that I choose partners who show up to love similarly to the way I do.

What are some things you don't want to have to ask for in a relationship?

The length of time that a person has been nonmonogamous does not necessarily determine how capable they are of having healthy polyamorous relationships.

Some people have been practicing nonmonogamy for many years but have done so in a way that didn't allow for growth and evolution in their relationships. They may have kept repeating the same patterns in each relationship they engaged in. Make sure that you aren't using a person's length of time being nonmonogamous as a secure indicator that they will be safe to be in a relationship with. Instead, ask about how they organize their relationships, ways that they have grown, lessons learned from previous relationships and what their nonmonogamy is like currently.

What are some indicators of polyamory maturity to you that aren't connected to the length of time a person has been practicing it?

Day 235

Don't put people on pedestals, because "gurus" are humans too. And learn to trust in your own inner wisdom and voice. Who better than you to guide and direct your path?

I am no guru by any stretch and you will never hear me position myself as one. I am not more evolved or enlightened than the average human being. I make mistakes, have a complex history of growth and challenge, and fully embrace my humanity. Most of the time, when I am writing these reminders, it's me talking to myself. ✸ Similarly, your teachers, educators and guides are human beings. Please remember that. And also remember that your own voice and wisdom are just as potent and worthy of consideration as anyone else's. Believe in your ability to guide yourself home. ✸ This advice may be more challenging if you struggle with mental illness or neurodivergence that affects your inner voice. If that voice tells you to self-harm or cause harm to others, please seek the help of a mental health professional.

What is your relationship with your inner voice like?

What is most important to me in my relationships with metamours is that they treat our shared partner well and don't intentionally interfere in my relationship with our partner.

I wish I could say that all of my metamour experiences have been positive but it's not true. I've had metamours who I deeply appreciate and metamours who I didn't care for in the slightest. I ask myself two things when it comes to sorting out my feelings about my metas:

1. Do I believe they care about our partner, respect them and treat them well?
2. Do I believe they respect the relationship I have with our partner, do not intentionally interfere with it and give it space to grow?

As long as the answer to those questions is yes, anything else I get from them is a bonus.

What are your expectations for your metamours? Are they realistic?

Being the partner without another partner can be hard and make showing up to your partners' other relationships more challenging. Think about how you would want your partner to show up to you if the roles were reversed.

I've been here many times. I'm here now. While this space is easier for me than it was when I was new to polyamory, it's still not what I would call easy. ❦ Being the only partner with one partner can be difficult. It's easier to reconcile what your partners are doing with others when you are also doing things with others. When that isn't the case, it can make the emotional struggles of nonmonogamy seem stronger. That's normal. ❦ I try to remember something a good friend told me: "The pendulum always swings back the other way." One day, it could be me with other partners and my partner struggling with just having me. The golden rule of showing up to others how you would want them to show up to you applies. And be honest about this being hard for you. There's no need to pretend you're having an easier time than you are. If you need some encouragement from your partner that someone will come along for you, too, ask for that.

What do you find uncomfortable about being the partner without another partner?

Nonmonogamy is an individual journey. Your path through it won't mirror the paths of your partners, even if you date the same person. Find your unique path through it.

Many of us get caught up in comparing our experience to our partners' experiences (or even those of friends), judging our "successes" and "failures" against theirs and wanting what they have. This is a deeply personal and individual path, even if you entered it as a part of a couple. ❧ Learn *your* way through it.

How has your pathway through polyamory differed from your partners'?

If you have partners who you allow to read your texts or other communication with other people, it is only fair that you tell those people that their conversations with you are not private.

I cannot tell you how common this is. Someone will be engaging with a person, thinking they are having private conversations with them, and then find out that the person's spouse or partner has been reading all of their messages or viewing pictures or videos sent. ❀ I don't let anyone read my messages and do not expect or even ask to read my partners'. My partners are grown adults who I trust to care about me and operate with my best interest at heart. I believe that the people they are with deserve to have privacy with them. I also respect the privacy of the people I'm with by keeping our communications between us. ❀ However, if you see nothing wrong with allowing your partners access to your correspondence with others, you need to let those people know that you are showing their messages to someone else before they begin corresponding with you so they can consent. If you find that you are having a hard time finding folks that are OK with that, examine why you need to share those messages in the first place.

What are your views on partners having access to your phone and reading your messages? Are you communicating those views to the people you interact with?

Ask clarifying relationship questions when dating and relating to folks in polyamory, especially with people who are partnered. Doing this early on can help you all to make informed relationship choices.

This is super important, especially for single and solo-polyamorous folks. It's important to ask the people you are connecting with how they organize their relationships so that you can make informed choices about the level of engagement you can realistically have and see if you are in alignment with what you want from one another. ❧ Consider asking whether they practice hierarchy in their relationships, if they have a veto agreement with any of their partners and whether they have any relationship agreements that will restrict or limit how you can move in your relationship. These are just the start. ❧ Don't go into these conversations with judgment, but recognizing that it's good to know what you're getting into. Things that aren't a problem for some folks are for others and the more you know, the more you know. There are many ways to practice nonmonogamy. Find folks who vibe with it in the same way as you vibe with it.

What questions are most important to you?

If you recently discovered that you are polyamorous and you are in a monogamous relationship, have empathy for your monogamous partner as they grieve the loss of their relationship with you as they knew it.

If you began a relationship with the expectation of mutual monogamy and then you change that expectation, it is normal and valid for your partner to struggle with that. As someone who cares for them, you should show some empathy for that struggle. ❧ Declaring that you are polyamorous after you have already been trying to date people or actually dating people without your partner's knowledge is cheating. Full stop. And declaring you are nonmonogamous and then plowing ahead at full speed with no regard for the feelings of your partner and demanding that they just "get on board" is cruel. ❧ It feels good to come into a deeper understanding of ourselves but we need to acknowledge the impact that such understanding has on the people we are in a relationship with. Yes, they can leave if they can't accept you, but you can also lovingly end the relationship with a person when you realize that you are no longer able to give them the relationship that they want with you. ❧ Heavy-handedly bludgeoning your partner with nonmonogamy is not OK.

If you entered into nonmonogamy with a partner, how was the experience? Was it gentle, abrupt or jarring?

Having compassion and empathy for your partners' struggles in nonmonogamy isn't the same as taking responsibility for their feelings or assuming guilt. It's acknowledging that they're in pain with care.

I read a book called *True Love* by Thich Nhat Hanh, a Buddhist monk and author. There's a mantra in it that you can practice with the people you love to work on being present for them. "Dear one, I know that you are suffering, that is why I am here for you," he writes. "Your presence is a miracle, your understanding of [their] pain is a miracle, and you are able to offer this aspect of your love immediately." ❧ I find that people really struggle with this in nonmonogamy. They have a hard time empathizing with their partners' struggles because they feel guilt for being the "cause" of the pain, they wish their partner felt differently or they struggle with their partner being uncomfortable about something that brings them joy. ❧ It is possible to empathize and be compassionate to our partners without assuming responsibility or guilt for what they are going through. You can simply acknowledge and validate that they are in pain and that you care about that. Don't try to "fix" it by changing what you are doing, and don't try to keep as much distance as possible because "you did nothing wrong." Offering compassion is just saying, "Hey, I see you're hurting and that matters to me."

What is the difference between expressing empathy for your partner's emotions and assuming responsibility for their feelings?

Day 243

Expressing to your partners the unique value they have to you and the specific ways you enjoy them as individuals helps them to feel special to you and can support them in not comparing themselves to the other special people in your life.

Don't compare your partners with others but do tell your partners the specific things you appreciate about them as individuals. Letting them know the unique ways they have value to you helps them to feel special to you and can combat any comparative thoughts they have about themselves and your other significant others. It also helps them to feel seen by you. ❧ Ask your partners to share with you the unique ways you matter to them, too.

What do you appreciate about each of your partners?
What do you think they appreciate about you?

Day 244

Being able to have open, honest, supportive conversations about STI status is necessary, both for your health and the health of everyone you're being sexual with. Let's end the stigma and shame around STIs.

We need to normalize having positive conversations about sexual health with our partners, new connections and ourselves. This includes things like keeping and sharing up-to-date test results, informing people about what safer sex practices you engage in, what levels of risk you're comfortable with (because all sexual activities carry some risk), what your status is, and when it's possible that your status may have changed or been compromised. Even a random hookup should include a conversation about status in a positive, nonjudgmental way. ✤ If someone can't show up to a conversation about sexual status, it's probably not a good idea to go past that point with that person for your own health and for the health of your partners. ✤ People with STIs aren't dirty or irresponsible. Let's change the language we use to talk about STIs so folks can feel empowered to talk honestly about them. ✤ Also, if you disclose that you have an STI and someone decides they don't want to continue dating you because of it, it's OK. (This has happened to me several times.) They get to decide what level of risk they feel comfortable with for their own body. And there will be other people who will enthusiastically say yes to you.

How have you personally challenged yourself to break down STI stigma and encourage honest and supportive conversations about it with your partners?

Just because you and a partner were compatible for monogamy together doesn't mean that you'll be compatible for nonmonogamy together.

This was definitely true for my marriage. We used to say that if we had met each other at this juncture and wanted to have nonmonogamous relationships, we probably wouldn't choose the other person. I believe many couples that transition from monogamy to nonmonogamy struggle with this. ❧ Just because you were able to make monogamy work together for a period of time, it doesn't mean that you will be able to navigate nonmonogamy together in a way that is compatible for both of you. As such, if you both decide that you want to continue to live nonmonogamously, it may be necessary to end the relationship. And that, though painful, is OK.

Have you ever experienced being compatible with a partner for monogamy but not being compatible with each other for nonmonogamy? If so, what happened to the relationship when you realized this?

**Don't push yourself to do things in nonmonogamy
that you aren't ready for simply to prove
a point to others or to yourself.**

We push ourselves to do things that we are not comfortable
with or emotionally ready for because we want to prove to
ourselves, to our partners, or to the polyamorous communities we are involved in that we are "good" polyamorous
people. That doesn't honor where we genuinely are at
in our journey and doing this often results in outcomes
that are worse than if we had just allowed ourselves
to be exactly where and who we are on our journey. ❀
Being a "good" polyamorous person isn't about being
the most compersive or the most accommodating of our
partners' other relationships. It's about being authentic
with ourselves and learning to respect the autonomy of
our partners while also respecting our own autonomy to
be and feel and do exactly what is healthiest for all parties
involved, and that absolutely should include ourselves.
You don't have a point to prove to anyone, including you.
You can just be real.

How have you tried to prove to yourself or others
that you were "good" at polyamory? Did you
push yourself too far in those situations?

Even if you can intellectually conceptualize that a person loves you, if you don't believe in your worthiness to be loved, you are going to struggle to feel it.

A dear friend once relayed to me that for the first time in their entire life, they felt surrounded by love and they were able to actually *feel* it. They said that before this, they could see evidence that they were loved by folks, and they could intellectually acknowledge that, but until they worked on their own belief in their worthiness of love, it never resonated like it should have because they struggled to feel it. ❀ Embrace that you are worthy of love. Full love. Whole love. Nourishing love. Accountable love. Healing love. Celebratory love. Affirming love. Compassionate love. Empathetic love. Enthusiastic love. Peaceful love. Free-flowing love. Desirable love. Gentle love. Self-love. ❀ From your partners, from your friends, from your family, from yourself. This is the love you deserve. ❀ Believe in and get acquainted with your self-worth so that you'll know what this all looks like for you. When you have it, you'll actually be able to rest in and enjoy it because you can feel it. ❀ You are worthy. I am too.

What makes you worthy of the love you want?

Nonmonogamy enables us to wipe the slate clean and gives us the opportunity to envision the kinds of relationships we want apart from societal prescriptions of what relationships should and shouldn't look like.

Nonmonogamy is a vast landscape of relationship opportunity, but many of us go into it carrying the old baggage of ideas about what relationships should or shouldn't look like from living in a monogamous society. We throw away the script only to try to apply it where it doesn't apply. I'm not just talking about romantic relationships, either, but all relationships. ❀ Maybe you want sexual friendships but nonsexual romantic relationships. Maybe you want your life partners to be platonic friends. Maybe you want spouses you don't live with. Maybe you want to parent with friends. Maybe you want to live in community with groups of people who hold various titles in your life. With consent and ethical behavior, anything is possible with the right folks. ❀ Polyamory opens a world of possibilities for what love authentically looks like for us, individually and collectively. Believe in the possibilities. Believe that you can craft the relationships that will best serve who you are. Believe in the truest version of love that you can envision for yourself.

What new relationship possibilities did you open up to when you became polyamorous?

It is possible to show empathy and concern for our partners' struggles in nonmonogamy without assuming guilt or responsibility for what they are feeling. You can hold that you aren't the creator of their feelings while caring that they are experiencing them.

It can be hard when our partners are challenged emotionally by something we're doing in nonmonogamy. It can be difficult to show concern and empathy because we may be feeling guilty or responsible for why they are uncomfortable. Instead of dealing with our own guilt or why we feel responsible for our partners' emotions, we can withhold concern or empathy for them so we don't feel badly about ourselves and what we're doing that may be causing them pain or discomfort. ❧ The reality is that discomforts will come in nonmonogamy and that's how growth happens. If you didn't violate any established agreements, you aren't wrong for what you did. And it is possible to show empathy and concern for our partners' struggles while holding on to our own autonomy to make choices that we want, even when those choices cause discomfort. It's saying, "Even though I'm connected to why you're uncomfortable, I know I'm not the cause of your discomfort. But I do care that you are in pain about this."

What barriers do you experience in showing empathy for your partners' emotions in nonmonogamy?

We don't have to be "perfect" to receive love. We deserve love even in moments where our individual humanity comes through.

We all have human moments, and we deserve to receive love even in these moments. ❦ We deserve to have relationships in which the other person can say, "I recognize that this person is a human being, and this is a moment when they are showing up as human, yet my love for them can still be present in this moment. My love does not require this person to always show up in a very specific way in order to receive it." ❦ That said, if your "human moments" cause harm or are abusive, the other person can and should remove themselves from their relationship with you. That doesn't mean that they do not love you, but they should love themselves enough to not allow themselves to continue to be harmed by you.

Do you deny yourself love because you aren't "perfect"? If so, in what ways?

Just because we don't "work" for someone, doesn't mean we fundamentally don't "work."

How does this relate to polyamory? Picture yourself in a relationship that is declining or perhaps even ending. As this is happening, your former partner may tell you all the ways that you don't "work" for them. You're too needy, too distant, too insecure, too emotional, not emotional enough, whatever it is. And as this is happening, you are aware that your former partner has relationships with others that are thriving. You might internalize this as you fundamentally not working instead of seeing it simply as you not working for that person. ❧ But look at all of your relationships. Sometimes the very thing that someone can't handle from us is something that another partner enjoys the most about us. We're all individuals. Do yourself a favor and change the narrative from "I don't work" to "I don't work for that person."

Have you ever internalized things about you that didn't work for another person as fundamental flaws within you? If so, what were those things?

It is a bright red flag when someone has nothing kind to say about their current partners and constantly complains to you about them.

I once went on a date with a new potential partner. We met online. They were attractive. Smart. They had some interesting pursuits. I noticed, however, that every time they mentioned their spouse, it was to say something critical or negative about them. They didn't make a single kind or loving or appreciative comment about their partner. It was a huge turnoff. ❀ Consider it a red flag when someone you are interested in or dating constantly speaks negatively about their partners. It creates discord between metamours and it creates mistrust. (What are they saying about *you* when you aren't around?). Plus, why is that person continuing to be with someone they are clearly so unhappy with? ❀ I understand the need to be honest about our relationship experiences and that people have low moments in their relationships, but someone who is constantly tearing down someone they claim to love? Ain't nobody got time for that. What gets me going are folks who are enthusiastically in love with their partners, the people who are open about their appreciation of who they love. Because that's how they'll love me if we get to that point.

What do you enjoy about people speaking highly of their partners? What does it say to you about them?

People get to decide how "out" they want to be about being polyamorous and who to be out to. It's important to consider your own preferences for being out and the preferences of those you are connecting to or in relationships with.

I'm completely out. My children, family, neighbors, friends, coworkers, even strangers—everybody knows I'm nonmonogamous. I once had a partner who wasn't out to their family. I didn't foresee it being a major issue, as I didn't need to be acknowledged by their family as their partner. However, their parents were their next-door neighbors. This placed me in some uncomfortable situations in which I had to hide our relationship and it eventually contributed to the relationship's end. ❀ It is important to understand your own personal preferences for being out and to discuss them with partners and potential ones. Dating someone more closeted than you may mean finding yourself in situations where you have to lie, hide or feel like a secret in some way. Being connected to someone more out than you may cause you to be exposed prematurely or inadvertently outed, which can cause problems. (I've inadvertently outed people and it wasn't fun.) Further, when you are already in a relationship with someone and you disagree on how out to be, it can cause a major rift. ❀ Have a conversation about "outness." Discuss what it looks like for you, what it looks like for them and if you align on how it looks for your relationship.

How out do you desire to be about being polyamorous? Do your partners' preferences differ from yours? How do you reconcile that?

There's nothing wrong with being polyamorous and having relationships with monogamous people, but if those people only tolerate your nonmonogamy, they are tolerating—not loving or appreciating—a major aspect of who you are, and that usually creates issues.

Mono/nonmono pairings are valid. I have seen instances where these situations work. But where they usually falter is in situations where the monogamous person is only tolerating the nonmonogamy of the other person. The monogamous person may say things like, "I love them, I just wish they weren't nonmonogamous," "I'm willing to put up with them being nonmonogamous because I want to be with them," or "I love them. I just don't love their non-monogamy." They may see their partner's nonmonogamy as a phase that they'll grow out of or believe that they can love the person enough to make them choose monogamy. ❧ On the flip side, some nonmonogamous people hope that their monogamous person will one day get on board with nonmonogamy or that they can love the person so well that eventually, they'll accept nonmonogamy. This rarely goes well from either vantage point. ❧ Whether nonmonogamy is a choice or intrinsically who you are, it is a major part of how you organize relationships, just like monogamy is a major part of how a monogamous person organizes relationships. When we are simply tolerating a major part of a person, it makes it hard to show up to fully loving them.

Have you ever dated someone who only tolerated your polyamory? If so, how did that make you feel?

If you notice your partner is showing up to another relationship in a way that you feel is lacking in your own relationship with them, don't make the disparity about the other relationship when addressing it.

Let's look at an example. Pat and Sam have been married for a long time. Sam has a newer partner, Gil. For years, Pat has tried unsuccessfully to get Sam to go dancing with them. Then Pat finds out that Sam has been going dancing on their dates with Gil. ❧ This hurts Pat's feelings, which is reasonable. They think, "Why is Sam willing to dance with Gil and not me? Sam must love Gil more. I'm going to tell Sam that it's unfair and demand they start dancing with me too." ❧ But Pat can choose a different response. They can give Sam the benefit of the doubt that they aren't trying to hurt them. Maybe it's the kind of dancing that Sam does with Gil that made them more open to trying it. Maybe Sam changed their mind about dancing but Pat was so used to being told no that they stopped asking. Maybe Pat previously showed up critically to Sam's attempts at dancing in a way Gil doesn't, which makes Sam feel safer. Rather than throw Sam's relationship with Gil in their face and demand to be treated the same, Pat can own that they are hurting, acknowledge that they also would like to dance with Sam and ask if they can find a dance experience they can enjoy together.

Have you ever experienced a similar scenario?
If so, how did you respond to it?

While it is not your partner's responsibility to fulfill you sexually, if it is important to you to have partners who enthusiastically desire to contribute to your sexual fulfillment, that is valid.

I often see posts in polyamory groups in which someone expresses that a partner has ceased or drastically reduced having sex with them. The responses often express that the person posting has no right to struggle with this. ❀ No one owes us sex, partner or not. And yes, we all have the right to revoke consent to sexual interaction at will. Asexual/graysexual persons are valid and deserve to have relationships where their sexuality is accepted and appreciated without coercion or pressure to engage in sex more than is comfortable for them. All of this is true. ❀ But if it is important to you to have partners who want to contribute to your sexual fulfillment, that is valid. And if someone you are with no longer wishes to interact with you in that way or to the degree you would like, you get to decide that the relationship no longer works for you. It doesn't make them or you a bad person. It just means you are no longer compatible. ❀ Many things can affect a person's desire for sex, including physiological problems, medications, emotional state, life stressors and more. Try to take these factors into account as you navigate this issue together.

How important is sex to you in your relationships?

You have every right to set boundaries if you are dealing with a metamour who is disrespectful to you or who is outright abusive.

I'm not talking about a metamour you struggle to get along with or who sometimes has challenging emotions about your relationship with their partner. I'm talking about a metamour who is passive aggressive or insulting, or who completely falls apart every time you're around or when you try to engage your partner. I'm talking about someone who violates your boundaries, is physically abusive (it happens), blames you for issues in their relationship with your partner or actively interferes with your relationship with your partner. This behavior is not OK and you have a right to draw a line between yourself and anyone who treats you that way and to expect both your metamour and your partner to honor that line. ❧ Polyamory can be challenging, but you are not someone's punching bag to work out their issues on. They are choosing to engage in nonmonogamous relationships and they need to do the work. They need to figure out their path in a way that minimizes harm to the people they are connected to, even if that connection is indirect. ❧ This situation disproportionately affects single and solo folks and folks who date married or nested people. These people are often made to feel like they don't have the right to decide not to interact with a person's primary partner or spouse.

Have you ever had an abusive or problematic metamour? If so, how did you handle it?

We don't get to decide for someone else what is or isn't permissible in a relationship or what is or isn't a forgivable offense.

Sometimes we can judge our partners—perhaps for forgiving another partner for something that we wouldn't forgive or for working with a partner on an issue that we wouldn't work with. We can also judge our partners for not being willing to get past something that we think they should get past, whether in their relationship with us or their relationships with others. ❧ The thing is, we don't get to decide for someone else what they should or shouldn't be willing to forgive, move past or let go of. We can't decide for our partners' other relationships what they should or shouldn't be willing to deal with. And we can't decide what someone should or shouldn't be willing to deal with from us, either. ❧ It can be challenging to see your partner treating others with more grace and forgiveness than you feel they do with you, but it's still not your role to decide what they should or shouldn't accept. ❧ This situation also becomes much more difficult when you have a partner dealing with clear abuse. You don't get to decide if they should deal with that, but you have every right to distance yourself from them or from their abusive relationship.

When your partners make decisions in other relationships that you don't understand, do you find yourself judging them or their choices? If so, what makes accepting their decisions without judgment challenging for you?

Someone breaking up with us is not necessarily a rejection of us. It is totally possible for someone to say, "I love you and what we have is real and also, it needs to end."

One of my favorite scenes from *Schitt's Creek* is the one in which Alexis and Ted break up for the final time. They had a wonderful relationship but continuing to be together would have forced one or both of them to give up on their dreams. Neither of them wanted that for themselves or the other. They wished each other well and ended their relationship with love. ❀ I deeply appreciated that the creators opted to show people choosing themselves and their hopes and dreams over maintaining a relationship that would cause them to sacrifice themselves. Love doesn't mean constantly having to sacrifice ourselves for the sake of keeping it, and I am here for the normalization of that message. ❀ Sometimes, it's not that someone doesn't love us anymore or that the connection is no longer there, but it's just not viable for them to continue to be with us. Ending the relationship could be an acknowledgment of their inability to meet our needs. Their life might be taking them in a direction that makes sustaining what they have with us impossible. Or it could be that that the sacrifices they would need to make to stay with us are too great. It doesn't mean that we were faulty partners, that the relationship was bad or that they no longer love us. It just means our time together in a particular way has come to an end.

Do you believe that love requires self-sacrifice? If so, in what ways?

The amount of time a person has been nonmonogamous does not determine how "safe" they are to be in a relationship with.

When I met my current partner, he was new to nonmonogamy and I had been practicing for much longer. Like many more experienced polyamorous folks, I had a measure of pause about dating someone less experienced in nonmonogamy. ❧ Often, folks new to this are still experiencing the usual early struggles or are unsure of what they want from nonmonogamy. If the newer person is part of a couple, there will likely be additional issues as they navigate the transition of opening up from monogamy. As a more experienced person, I have already gone through all of those things and knowing I may have to endure these challenges again by proxy through someone I'm dating isn't too appealing. ❧ However, with my current partner, I noticed that even though he was new to nonmonogamy, his ability to navigate it and the way he managed his relationships allowed for me to feel safe. Conversely, I have seen people with years of experience in nonmonogamy acting in ways that put me off entering into a relationship of any kind with them. ❧ Time in nonmonogamy doesn't guarantee safety, and the assumption that it does often trips people up. When making partner choices, it's best to take your time and observe who someone is and how they operate.

How do you feel about people new to polyamory?
Do you automatically assume a relationship
with them will be challenging?

There's a difference between polyamory as a state of being and polyamory as a choice. Both are valid and need to be respected, acknowledged and understood.

For some people, polyamory is as much an identity as their sexuality or ethnicity. Discovering polyamory can feel like a homecoming for them. For others, polyamory is a choice. It is how they choose to organize their relationships, exercise personal freedom or align with their personal love politics. Neither way is better or worse—they're just different. ❧ There is sometimes misunderstanding between folks for whom it is an identity and folks for whom it is a choice. These differing folks may even be in a relationship with each other. Naturally polyamorous people can sometimes struggle to understand the challenges that polyamorous-by-choice folks face and may say things like, "Why do you continue to do this if it's so hard for you? Maybe you're not polyamorous." This can be incredibly invalidating for the person hearing it. ❧ On the flip side, polyamorous-by-choice people may not understand a naturally polyamorous person's deep need to be themselves. They may ask for restrictions or changes to the way they practice nonmonogamy and not understand why the naturally polyamorous person struggles so hard with those asks. To the naturally polyamorous person, this can feel like being asked to not be themselves. ❧ Whatever your experience of polyamory is, be firm in that understanding of yourself and choose relationships with folks who also understand and accept this about you.

Is polyamory a choice or an identity for you?

If you can't identify what the benefit of polyamory is for you personally, you are going to struggle with it. Polyamory is a deeply personal journey and for the greatest success, you need to connect to your own reasons for doing it.

Other folks' reasons can't be your reasons because other folks can't live your polyamorous life for you. If you are doing it for others or for the reasons given to you by others, it will be hard to see it as genuinely worthwhile, especially when things are challenging. When things get difficult, knowing why polyamory is important to you can carry you through the challenges you face.

What are your personal reasons for engaging in polyamory? What makes it worthwhile for you?

If your partner has requested that you halt or limit your interactions with others to support them, and you have chosen to honor that request, don't throw them under the bus by blaming your decision on them. Be accountable for your choices.

It's the difference between saying, "My partner is struggling with my relationship with you and making me break up with you," and saying, "My partner is struggling with my relationship with you and has asked me to end it and I am choosing to support them by doing so." ❀ The first version places all the blame on your partner. The second owns that you have chosen to grant their request. If you choose to change or end your relationships with others for the sake of a partner, you need to own that it was your choice to do so. And if someone changes or ends their relationship with you at the request of a partner, understand that the person you were interacting with made their choice.

Has a partner ever blamed you for a choice they made in another relationship? If so, how did that make you feel?

Being sexually liberated isn't about the number of sexual partners or experiences you have but about allowing yourself to freely exist in your authentic sexuality.

You can be an asexual person who is sexually liberated or a self-proclaimed slut who is not sexually liberated. Sexual liberation isn't about the number of sexual experiences or partners you have but about operating in the most free expression of your authentic sexuality. ❀ Sexual liberation for you and your partners will look different. If we aren't careful, we can sometimes "slut shame" or "prude shame" our partners because their engagement with sex doesn't mirror ours. Let them work out their sexualities for themselves and focus on your own.

What does sexual liberation mean for you?

Day 265

Our past experiences with our families, relationships and life in general can inform how we show up in our current relationships, but they aren't excuses for poor behavior.

I came from a very abusive home. So, when I engaged in abusive behavior in my own relationship, it made sense why. It didn't excuse the behavior, though. It was my responsibility to recognize the pattern that was set for me and to break it within myself. ❀ We didn't have control over what we endured in our families when we were children, what previous partners did to us or how we were harmed by life, and those experiences can and will shape how we engage in relationships, in both positive and negative ways. However, we do have control over our current behavior and how much we allow those experiences to influence what we do. ❀ So, yeah, you may have gotten cheated on by previous partners and that sucks, but it doesn't excuse you tyrannically dictating that your current partners outline their every move to you because you struggle to trust people. Past hurts provide an explanation for current fears, but they don't excuse unhealthy behavior toward others in response to those fears. It's our job to heal so that we don't perpetuate harm toward others from our place of pain. We have to stop being hurt people so we can stop hurting people.

Do any of your past experiences impact your behavior in the present? How are you working on that?

Some wisdoms will only come from practice and experience. Learn to be OK with making mistakes, trying things you're not sure about and being gracious with yourself and your partners as you figure out what works for you.

Wisdoms can came from the school of hard knocks. I made mistakes, and I learned hard lessons as a result. I had to grow, change and be flexible with myself and others, and I had to navigate all of that with grace and compassion. ❀ You can't cheat time and experience. You have to be OK with stumbling along the way, not getting it right all the time and learning as you go. All the preparation in the world won't be able to substitute for actual experience and doing the work of finding your own answers. It's all part of the dance.

How can you be more patient with yourself and your growth in polyamory?

It is not our partners' responsibility to make us OK with their choices in nonmonogamy. It's important to have partners who genuinely care that we're mostly OK with what they're doing, but it's not their job to make us comfortable.

This is the difference between saying, "In order for me to be OK with what you're doing, you have to do this, this and this" and saying, "I'm trying to be OK with this. This is what I think I need from you in order to support me. Are you willing to do that?" ❧ While I believe it is important that we have folks in our lives who genuinely care that we are OK in our nonmonogamous experience with them (not always comfortable, but OK), it is not our partners' job to manage our emotions or fix our feelings, especially when that comes at the price of things they are either incapable of or unwilling to do. ❧ It is our job to create our "OKness." Our loving partners can support us as we manage that, but it is our responsibility to ourselves to do inner work to restore our sense of peace about our experience.

How do you help yourself feel OK when dealing with a challenging experience in polyamory?

Nonmonogamy is not greedy. There is nothing greedy about wanting as much love and pleasure as you can enjoy and also wanting that for the people you love and care about.

Monogamy is based in the idea that romantic love is a scarce resource, so we should find "the one" and be content with that. If that's your viewpoint on romantic love, that is your prerogative, but folks who wish to live lives of abundant romantic love and/or sexual fulfillment are not greedy. They just have a different belief. ❧ It is not greedy to want multiple partners. It is not greedy to want a variety of sexual partners and experiences. It is not greedy to want as many of the exact kind of relational experiences you desire with as many people as you can have them with. ❧ You are worth abundance. You are worth total fulfillment. You are worth a cup overflowing with love and pleasure.

Do you feel greedy for being polyamorous? If so, why?

Learn to sit with your uncomfortable feelings and the thoughts that come up around them. Those thoughts hold clues to figuring out where the feelings are coming from and finding the origin is how you'll best address them.

This means not just acknowledging that we are feeling jealous or insecure or envious but asking why we're feeling that way. Why am I feeling so crunchy about my partner going on a date with their new interest? What is it about this person that triggers my insecurities and which insecurities are they triggering? Why do I feel like I want what I see my partner has in their relationship with someone else? ❧ Feelings are signals. They are messages from our most vulnerable selves that give us information about what is going on with our inner experience of our outer reality. Once you've identified that a feeling is present, the next step is to sit with your thoughts around the feeling to find out what its message is to you. When you have that information, you can then begin to piece together what is going on inside and how best to address it. ❧ This is especially important if you want to change your emotional responses to things you experience in nonmonogamy—you're going to have to get down to the root of where those emotions come from so you can heal what you need to heal, update your relationship beliefs and values to the new paradigm you're working with and change your own story about what it means to be in relationship.

What does sitting with your emotions accomplish for you?

Day 270

Just because you find someone attractive or interesting, it doesn't mean you need to act on it.

In the beginning of my journey, I sought to engage in a sexual way with every person I felt even a remote attraction to. And frankly, I am sure it was off-putting to many folks. ❧ I am just now learning how to interact differently with folks who I feel an attraction to. They may even feel an attraction to me, but I don't necessarily need to act on that or assert that it is what's going on. Just because I find someone physically appealing and may even enjoy their company and personality, they aren't necessarily someone I need to try to engage with sexually or romantically. I am learning that there are other things that I need for that to happen, like understanding their values, ideologies and who they are as a whole. I want to know a person and understand how their life is organized before I decide if they are someone I wish to engage with in those ways.

What factors do you consider before you act upon an attraction?

You can be a monogamous person and not desire to control your partner. You can be a nonmonogamous person and still desire to control your partners. Controlling behavior is not exclusive to monogamy.

There's a myth that people desire monogamy because they wish to control and limit their partner's behavior, but this idea doesn't really make sense. A monogamous person isn't controlling their partner's behavior by the relationship orientation—their partner is making the choice to be exclusive to them. ❀ I've also known plenty of nonmonogamous people who operate in very controlling and limiting ways with their partners. A person being nonmonogamous does not automatically mean they have released their desire for control of their partners. ❀ Toxic relationship behaviors persist in all relationship orientations, so making generalized assumptions isn't wise.

What controlling behaviors have you had to unlearn in your relationships?

It can be difficult to inadvertently receive information that you feel should have come directly from your partner. Try to remember to pause, calm down and get the whole story before you decide to be upset at your partner about it.

I used to have a partner who I regularly felt surprised by in nonmonogamy. It wasn't malicious and their intent was not to conceal information from me. Rather, it was a combination of differing privacy needs, misalignment on what we both considered relevant information and their fear of my more emotional responses. This dynamic caused a lot of issues throughout the course of our relationship. ❁ When I was surprised by information, I reminded myself of this saying: "Before you get upset, get curious." I would try to remember to pause, calm down and ask my partner why they didn't directly share the information. Perhaps they thought they told me but it wasn't clear to me. Perhaps they were waiting for the right time and I found out before they had a chance to get to me. Perhaps they, or even I, wasn't aware that it was information I wanted to come from them. Perhaps it was information they didn't feel they "had" to tell me directly. ❁ It is totally valid to be upset about feeling blindsided, but that doesn't necessarily mean you need to be upset with your partner for it. Do a little research before you decide how to handle it.

Have you ever felt upset by information you inadvertently received in polyamory? How did that make you feel? How did you respond?

Day 273

While it can be liberating to live your nonmonogamous truth, barreling forward without care, compassion and consideration of existing partners isn't kind or loving.

It is unkind to bludgeon your partner with nonmonogamy with little or no concern for how they feel, no empathy for their grief at the loss of their monogamous relationship, no acknowledgement of their need for adjustment time or no space to make their own changes to the relationship to care for themselves. ❧ Yes, deciding to live your nonmonogamous truth can feel liberating and like a weight removed from your shoulders, but steamrolling your partners with nonmonogamy because you don't wish to be "shackled" by them anymore is heartless. If you love and care about them, you should be compassionate in your approach to navigating nonmonogamy. They may not have wanted a nonmonogamous relationship but are likely trying their best to accept who you are and give you freedom. If you can't do this, have the loving kindness to end the relationship with them so you can live the life you desire without causing harm. ❧ People experience legitimate trauma from other people's heavy-handed nonmonogamous ways.

Have you ever felt like a partner was being heavy-handed with you in their navigation of nonmonogamy? If so, what was that experience like for you?

Couples entering nonmonogamy together often struggle with pacing. One may want to go full speed while the other wants to be more cautious. It's important to accommodate the needs of each person and try to find a comfortable pace for both.

I often see couples struggle to pace the transition into nonmonogamy. One person wants to plow ahead while the other has reservations and wants to be more cautious, often due to feeling less secure in the relationship. This is challenging to navigate because one person can feel weighed down and one can feel as if they are being uncomfortably dragged along. ❦ It's important that couples be mindful of attuning to each other's needs for how fast or how slow to transition into nonmonogamy and make sure that they honor their desires while also making accommodations for the desires of their partners. Plowing along at full speed with a partner who is more hesitant can cause the more cautious person injury. Taking your time while with a partner who is ready to move forward can cause the faster person to feel restricted and boxed in. Finding a comfortable pace that works for both parties can be the difference between a successful transition and one that is littered with conflict and pain. ❦ This is one of the benefits of entering nonmonogamy as a single person—you only have to consider how fast or slow you wish to navigate it.

If you entered into polyamory with a partner, was pacing an issue for you? If so, how did you navigate it?

You are not obligated to manage your partners' other relationships or the space they create for their other relationships, especially if that comes at the expense of your own relationship needs.

My first polyamorous relationship was a triad. I remember at times being so concerned about making sure my partners were getting time together and that their relationship was working well that I felt like they were at Disneyland together having a great time and I was the one behind the scenes working the rides. I'd deny my own needs with my partners, or feel bad for even having needs, because I didn't want to be "in the way" of their relationship. ❀ Our partners are adults and it's their responsibility to manage their time with others, set boundaries and learn to communicate when they're available and to whom. We can spend so much time worrying about not being in the way of their other relationships that we deny our reasonable needs from our partners. ❀ It's important to remain present in your relationships with your partners and let them work out their relationship with others. You can respect their relationships with others but the management of them is their work. While I believe it is important to care that their other relationships are functioning well, when that care comes at your own expense, it's not sustainable. It also takes away the opportunity for your partners to develop necessary skills for navigating multiple relationships.

Why do you think it's important to learn to let your partners manage their own relationships? Is that something you find easy or hard to do?

It's OK to ask your partner to express their new-relationship energy somewhere else, to ask them to be aware of it and mitigate its effects on you and to ask that they be more intentional about reassuring you as they are experiencing it.

New-relationship energy (NRE) is that bubbly, euphoric feeling you might get when you're in a new exciting relationship. It can be difficult if your partner is in the throes of NRE with someone else, especially if your relationship with them is much older and those feelings faded a long time ago. Many polyamorous relationships suffer damage due to mismanagement of NRE. ❧ You are not "bad" at nonmonogamy if you find it difficult to engage with your partner's NRE with another person or ask for consideration when your partner is experiencing it. And if you are the partner experiencing NRE, don't get so swept up in it that you are inconsiderate or insensitive to your other partners in your excitement. No one is trying to rain on your parade. Share your excitement with other people and endeavor to make all of your partners feel like you are enthusiastic about your relationships with them.

How do you experience your partners' NRE? Are you excited with them or is it challenging for you to witness?

Polyamory has its challenges and difficulties, like most things in life. Something being hard at times doesn't make it not worth doing if it truly matters to you.

People often respond to folks talking about the challenges of nonmonogamy by saying things like, "Why put yourself through that?" "If it's that hard, why do it? Doesn't seem worth it," or "You seem to be struggling with this. Why not give it up because clearly, it's too hard for you." ❀ Plenty of things that are hard are worthwhile to the people they have value to. Polyamory is no different. While it shouldn't be continuously hard, challenges are unavoidable at times. That doesn't mean it's not worth doing. If polyamory is important to you, you accept the hard with the easy, the challenging with the simple. ❀ It's also OK to ask someone not to invalidate your polyamorous experience when you share your challenges with it.

Have people responded to you sharing your difficulties in polyamory in invalidating ways? If so, how?

Polyamory doesn't cause people to break up. Rather, it brings awareness to ways people aren't compatible with each other that they may not have discovered being monogamous together. Stop blaming polyamory for relationships ending.

When my marriage ended, some folks attributed it to the fact that we became nonmonogamous. "See? It's because y'all became polyamorous. That's what destroyed it," I heard. I find this response interesting because monogamous relationships end all the time and no one blames monogamy. Polyamory didn't end my marriage. Truthfully, I don't know if there's an alternate reality somewhere where we didn't become nonmonogamous and broke up five years earlier. ❧ Honestly, there is no one reason why we're not together anymore other than recognizing that a romantic relationship is not the best choice for us at this time. That's it. That's it for any relationship that ends. Many people need something to blame for why a relationship "failed" instead of just seeing it as the relationship reaching its limit of viability. ❧ Polyamory can't rip up a relationship any more than it can save a relationship.

Have you ever had someone blame polyamory for one of your relationships ending? Have you ever felt like polyamory was to blame for a relationship ending?

Nonsexual romantic relationships exist, and they are not "just friendships." People are allowed to want romantic relationships that aren't sexual. Don't assume that nonmonogamy is only about folks wanting more people to have sex with.

Asexual and graysexual folks exist and there are many folks who desire nonsexual romantic relationships. There is nothing wrong with this desire. If this is what you want, communicate that to the people you are engaging with so you can find folks in alignment with this type of relationship.

Do you now or have you ever had a nonsexual romantic relationship? If so, how was that experience for you?

What best serves our partners, relationships and ourselves is only agreeing to provide things that we are truly willing to give. Agreeing to make accommodations and considerations that we don't want to breeds resentment and our partners can feel that even though we're giving them what they want.

Imagine that one of your partners asks you to refrain from engaging in public displays of affection with another partner at an event you are all attending together. You reluctantly agree to grant this request. At the event, your other partner notices you aren't being affectionate with them and when you tell them why, they become upset. Then you're upset because you didn't want to do this in the first place. ❧ Instead of agreeing to things you don't wish to, try being honest with your partner and asking if there's something else you can both come up with that gives them what they need and you are willing to provide. Getting to the root of why your partners are requesting certain accommodations can offer insight into what kind of support they are truly seeking and can give you ideas for how you can help them that don't feel too restrictive or limiting to you. ❧ You can say something like, "I'm unwilling or unable to accommodate this request but I am willing to find ways to help support you feeling cared for. Can you tell me why you feel you need this specific thing and what's behind it so I can see if there's something else I can do that addresses your need and I can enthusiastically agree to?"

Has a partner ever felt resentment toward you because they agreed to something you asked for that they didn't genuinely want to do? How did you address the resentment?

Our partners are allowed to date monogamous people. It may make you uncomfortable when they do, and your concerns about this are valid, but they aren't wrong for choosing to do so.

Poly/mono pairings are valid. Some polyamorous folks have no issue with dating monogamous folks, and some monogamous folks have no issue dating polyamorous folks, but some nonmonogamous people struggle with their partner's choice to date monogamous people. They might worry that the monogamous person will struggle too much with their partner's other relationships, cause unnecessary drama or attempt to "steal" their partner and lure them back to monogamy. ❧ Those things do happen, and there's less opportunity for them to occur if your partners solely date nonmonogamous people. But truthfully, plenty of nonmonogamous people create unnecessary drama in relationships and attempt to "take" partners. I think it's more important that our partners pick good folks, whether they're monogamous or not. If you trust your partner's judgment and their commitment to your relationship, you don't have to worry about who they're dating, monogamous or not.

What are your thoughts about you or your partners dating monogamous people?

Polyamory can raise the bar and increase the standard for all other relationships. Nonmonogamy can show us what we truly want and sometimes show us that the relationships we currently have don't measure up.

In nonmonogamy, it is not uncommon to find yourself in a relationship that so genuinely meets your needs and is so fulfilling that you realize that what you wanted was possible but that you may just have been with the wrong folks. You can find yourself in a relationship that raises the standard for what you're willing to accept moving forward. It may change your outlook on the standard of care you deserve, how you wish to feel in your relationships and what you want your relationships to look like. ❀ When this happens, it can be tough on the other relationships you have. Do you work with your partners to see if the relationships can meet that standard? Do you accept what you were already receiving? Do you decide these relationships will never be what you want them to be and move on? Only you can make those choices, but it's OK and an act of self-love to update your standards when you realize you deserve what you truly want.

Have you ever experienced a bar-raising relationship? If so, what made it different from your other relationships?

When we experience a breakup in polyamory, it's normal to respond by becoming withdrawn in our other relationships, or by becoming more anxious. The pain of a connection severing can color our perception so that all connection feels unsafe.

Once, after one of my partners broke up with me, I began to contemplate ending all of the relationships I was in. I felt broken and damaged and like I needed to retreat into myself and draw away from love, even though my relationship with my other partner was amazing. I also noticed that I was afraid to connect to new people. Crushes felt scary. The thought of dating made me sad. Even people expressing interest in me didn't have the same effect that it used to. ❀ It's OK to be tender after a breakup and to struggle with connection when one happens. It's normal to feel the need to withdraw or to cling to other relationships. It makes sense that you want to shield yourself from another loss. The loss of a relationship can make us fear the loss of all relationships and that fear alters our sense of security. ❀ Talk to your partners if this is happening to you. Let them know that it isn't about them but about you being in a tender space of loss and your sense of security in relationships being shaken.

When experiencing a breakup in polyamory, do you feel the urge to withdraw from your other relationships? If so, why?

Parents often struggle with whether they should disclose to their children that they are polyamorous, and when. To me, when the decision to keep it from them enters the space of insulting your children's intelligence, it's probably a good idea to be honest with them.

I told my kids when they were eight, eight and five. My husband and I initially decided they didn't need to know, but when our partner was around, it became apparent to me that they would likely pick up on the fact that this person wasn't like mom and dad's other friends. Now, we've spent more of their lives being nonmonogamous than we did being monogamous. It's normal for them now. ❧ If and when to tell your children you are polyamorous is a personal choice and there are definitely circumstances where not telling them is necessary. However, when it gets to the point of your children being able to figure out that something "different" is going on, you should probably find an age-appropriate way to tell them. When kids find out about it on their own or learn about it inadvertently, they are usually more upset about being lied to than they are about the nonmonogamy. Children are far more perceptive and intelligent than we give them credit for. ❧ Hiding or lying about your nonmonogamy implies that it is something to be ashamed of. There is nothing shameful about being polyamorous.

If you have children, are you out to them about being polyamorous? Why or why not?

When considering the kind of nonmonogamous life you want to cultivate, make sure you choose partners who can support what you want and that you also consider if what you want is possible with the relationship(s) you currently have.

Frequently, people will imagine an ideal polyamorous life but consistently make choices that don't support that ideal. Or they will interact with others to ensure that they can offer a relationship that matches their ideals, but their life circumstances or current relationship setup doesn't allow for them to be able to deliver on those promises. ❧ So, setting someone up to expect a kitchen-table poly relationship with you when you know you have a partner who has a history of hostility toward your other partners isn't dealing in the reality of what you can reasonably offer a person. Knowing you want a hierarchy and choosing to be "primary" with someone who is a relationship anarchist will probably result in frustration for you. It's good to know what we want, but that knowledge is ineffective if we aren't applying it practically to our lives. ❧ There's what we want and then there's what we got. Acknowledging both is what will ultimately give you the ability to bring them into alignment with each other.

How are your current choices in alignment with your polyamorous ideals?

It's important to remember that our metamours are people who want the same thing that we want— to enjoy their relationships with our partners. Having empathy and compassion and attempting to understand our metamours goes a long way.

One of the best pieces of advice I've gotten in nonmonogamy is to assume good intent about my partners. I have also found this to be true about our metamours. We can often take things personally or choose to feel like metamours are adversaries or competitors for our partners, or we can build them up to be archetypes that set off our insecurities instead of humanizing them and seeing them as flesh-and-blood people who just want to be cared for and loved by someone they value. ❧ Whether you have or desire a close relationship with your metamour or not, you can still see them as a human being and still endeavor to have compassion and empathy for them as your partner's partner. It is also important to not personalize things that your metamour does. For example, they aren't asking your partner for more time because they want to take time away from you—they just want more time together. They're not feeling envious of your partner going on a trip with you because they don't want them to go anywhere with you—they are just a person with their own wants, needs and insecurities who is trying to be cared for, just like you are.

How do you foster compassion and empathy for your metamours?

It's OK to want monogamy. It's OK to end a relationship because you don't want to be nonmonogamous. It's OK to return to monogamy. It's OK to fluctuate between monogamy and nonmonogamy. It's OK to attempt nonmonogamy and decide it isn't for you.

We need to stop shaming folks for wanting monogamy, returning to monogamy, ending relationships with folks because they want nonmonogamy, being poly/mono flux or giving nonmonogamy a try and then deciding it isn't for them. I get tired of nonmonogamous folks acting like people want monogamy or can't handle nonmonogamy because of some kind of personal failing or because they don't want to "grow" or "do the work" or because they are less evolved in their beliefs about love. That's bullshit. ❀ Just like you have every right to be nonmonogamous, folks have every right to want to be monogamous.

What feelings come up when you consider returning to monogamy or a partner returning to monogamy?

Engaging in open relationships will be hard for you if you have a closed mind or maintain a rigid sense of self.

Expect to have your ideas challenged. Expect your and your partners' needs and wants and ideas to change and evolve. Expect to find ways that you have to grow and change. Having an open mind and seeking to be a person who is flexible and pliable helps to make your nonmonogamous pathway less hard and painful.

How have you have had to stretch in polyamory?

We don't owe our partners every accommodation they ask us for simply because they asked.

Sometimes, our partners ask for accommodations in nonmonogamy that we have no problem providing for them and can happily agree to. Other times, we are asked for things that we are either incapable of doing or unwilling to do. In those instances, you have every right to say, "No, I don't wish to or cannot accommodate you in that way." ❧ Maybe your partner asked that you only post pictures of them on social media and no other partners, or that you refrain from certain sex acts with anyone else. Perhaps they asked you to make them your primary or to agree to a waiting period before sleeping with new potential partners. It's not wrong for your partner to ask for these things and if you want to agree to them, that's your choice. But if you know that you can't or don't want to limit yourself in a particular way, it's much better to be honest about that instead of resentfully agreeing to provide an accommodation you either can't or don't want to give out of a sense of obligation. ❧ You can say, "I am unable/unwilling to provide this, but I do care about your need for it. Can we come up with something else that I can enthusiastically offer you that accommodates a similar need?"

Do you feel a sense of obligation to grant every accommodation your partners ask for? If so, why?

We all have the right to make changes to the relationships we are in as it suits our needs and desires, but we must accept that our partners also have the right to make their own changes in response to those adjustments.

Someone will make a change to their relationship and then be completely bewildered or upset about their partner responding to that change with one of their own. We sometimes forget that relationships are like painting a picture with another artist or artists. It's not just about what you think will look good but about collaborating with the other individuals so that every contributor feels their desires are represented. ❀ Say you decide you don't want to live with your partner. Or you no longer want a sexual relationship with them. Or you don't want to have a "primary" partner. All of these desires are valid, but it's also valid for a person you previously shared those things with to struggle with those changes and want to make changes of their own in response. ❀ You may see the change as something that will ultimately feel better for you both but if that doesn't match their picture, they get to make their own changes to bring the relationship into alignment with what they think will bring them fulfillment. If you want grace and understanding as you shift, you must also be willing to give them the same.

What emotions come up when you think about your partners making changes to your relationship, perhaps changes that you don't want?

There's saying what we mean and then there's meaning it how we said it. It can be difficult to reconcile these when our emotions are activated. Honesty is important, but so is communicating kindly, constructively and compassionately.

I may have something I need to express to my partner, and I want to be honest with them, but in the height of my emotions about it, it doesn't always come out the way I want it to. It's important to tell the truth about how we feel but to also remember that we want our truth to be heard and received. It can be hard for our partners to really hear something if we communicate in ways that are sharp, sarcastic, unkind or insulting. ❧ You can say to your partner, "I'm concerned about the people you pick to partner with" or you can say, "I can't stand the people you choose to date—you have poor taste." Both statements have the same intent, but which one do you think your partner will respond to better? Taking the time to choose our words wisely can be the difference between an issue moving toward resolution or becoming further exacerbated. ❧ Acknowledge when you communicate without care. Own when you speak from the place of heightened emotion and cause hurt. Don't dismiss it by saying something like, "I was just being honest." You can be honest and kind or honest and unkind. Which one matters to you?

What does "kind honesty" mean to you?

How someone behaves in a relationship with others isn't necessarily a solid indicator of how they will behave in relationship with you. A person can treat one person well and treat another poorly.

In polyamory, it's normal to observe a person's relationships to see what kind of partner they are. But how someone shows up in other relationships isn't a guarantee that you'll be treated the same way. Remember that every relationship is unique and the interaction you have with someone could be very different from the interactions they have with others. It's best to focus on your experience of a person to gauge if what they are offering you works for you or not. ❧ Just because someone is treating you poorly or wonderfully, it doesn't mean that that's how they're treating their other partners. Oftentimes, folks question or even judge their metamours' difficulties with their shared partner by saying things like, "They're so amazing to me. They can't possibly be treating you like that." A person can be a saint to you and an utter asshole to someone else. Newer partners often struggle to empathize with older partners' issues with their shared partner for this very reason.

Do you look at how a person treats their partners as an indicator of how they'll treat you? If so, what behaviors do you take note of?

Your partners can't make promises for their future selves. They can't promise you that the relationship will never change, that they'll never change or that their feelings will never change. And you can't make any of those promises to your partners either.

Our partners can't promise us that they are always going to want to remain married or nested, that they'll want to maintain a hierarchy or stay poly-fidelitous, that they'll want to continue in a sexual and/or romantic relationship with us or that they'll always desire us in the same way that they did when they embarked on their relationship with us. People change, their feelings change, their needs change. The same thing is true for us—we change, our feelings change, our needs change. Sometimes our relationships can weather those changes but sometimes they can't. Holding on too rigidly to people and their feelings staying the same or our relationships with them never changing makes acceptance much harder when the inevitable changes occur.

Did you make relationship promises in the past that have changed for you as your desires changed? If so, what were they?

Before you get disappointed about your partner(s) not being supportive about your new relationship with someone else, ask yourself if your movements with the new person fostered an environment for your partners to be encouraging about it.

Sometimes, it's not your partners trying to rain on your parade but your new-relationship energy affecting your consistency in your older relationships. It's normal to get caught up in the rapture of an exciting new love but if we let those frenzied early feelings of elation impact how we treat our older relationships, it is highly likely that our partners will struggle to be supportive of us, no matter how much they may wish to. ❧ If your partners are particularly struggling with your new relationship, examine your behavior to see if you've been slacking in your relationship with them or lacking in care for their needs. You could even ask if they feel as if you've forgotten about them in your excitement with your new relationship. You may uncover that you got carried away and left your partners feeling deserted. ❧ If you want partners who are supportive of your relationships with others, it's important to create an environment where they can be. You can do that by demonstrating appreciation of all of your relationships.

Have you ever gotten carried away with new-relationship energy? If so, what impact did it have on your other relationships?

It's difficult to find ourselves in situations where we recognize that our partners did nothing wrong and yet still not like what they did and feel uncomfortable about it. Acknowledge that both are valid and both can exist.

Imagine that your partner went out on a date and told you they'd text you when they got home but you didn't hear from them that evening. When you spoke to them the next morning, you found out that they didn't send you a message because they stayed over at their date's place and it slipped their mind. While your partner wasn't wrong, you wish they had sent you a message at some point in the evening and also feel a little jarred by the fact that their date with the person progressed so quickly. ❧ When this happens, it can be hard to reconcile what the response is. There's nothing you can pinpoint that your partner needed to change about their behavior and yet you're having uncomfortable feelings about what happened. The knowledge that your partner wasn't wrong doesn't change how you feel, which can then make you feel like you're wrong for having your feelings. ❧ The reality is that your partner wasn't wrong for exercising their freedom and you aren't wrong for feeling uncomfortable about it. One doesn't need to cancel out or change the other. There's space for both to exist.

Have you ever felt discomfort but no one did anything "wrong"? If so, which part was hardest for you to come to terms with?

The best relationships are the ones where we can be as close to who we authentically are as possible and still be in harmony with the people we are walking alongside in life.

I once appeared on the Normalizing Nonmonogamy podcast and was given the prompt, "The best relationships are ____." My answer was that the relationships that feel best to me are the ones where I feel free to be exactly who I genuinely am, and that who I am is complementary and harmonious with who the other person genuinely is—relationships where I am at peace with myself and I am at peace with my partner. ❦ If I have to hide myself, truncate myself, or be someone I'm not in order to remain in harmony with someone, I am out of harmony with myself. Fiercely holding on to my authenticity helps me more easily identify who can truly journey alongside me because I am giving people the truth about the kind of walking partner I am. If who I genuinely am creates disharmony in a relationship, then it's best we change course until we can return to harmony or go our separate ways so we can each find peace to be ourselves.

How do you cultivate safe space for authenticity in yourself and others you are in relationships with?

Rejecting someone, breaking up with them or turning down the kind of relationship they want with you isn't easy and can cause a lot of anxiety. Still, have the courage to be honest and the compassion to be kind with that honesty.

I had a conversation with a friend about various forms of rejection. We were discussing all of the insensitive, unkind and cowardly ways people disconnect from or shift connections with folks. So much so, that we considered hosting a workshop on how to reject people with kindness. ❀ No, you don't owe anyone any kind of courtesy and yes, you are allowed to alter or sever a connection at will and in the way that feels safest for you. Still, I often find that folks choose methods that are uncaring to the person on the other end of their decision—methods that they themselves would find hurtful if done to them—simply because they didn't choose courage in stating their desires. ❀ It's not easy to hurt someone you care about, disappoint folks or let someone down, but that doesn't mean you get to do it in a way that is unkind, uncaring, dishonest or avoidant. Have the courage to state your genuine desires. Understand that you may be causing a person pain but that you aren't destroying them. Ultimately, being honest with them is the kindest thing you can do. Think of how you would want someone to treat you if the shoe was on the other foot.

Has anyone rejected you in a way that was unkind or cowardly? If so, how did that make you feel? What do you wish they had done differently?

Maintaining a spirit of curiosity in nonmonogamy is vital to navigating it successfully. Before you get upset, get curious.

When navigating nonmonogamy, it is imperative to break down the internalized assumptions about love and relationships that we inherit from our cis-heteronormative monogamous culture, family, media, etc. To do so, we must maintain a spirit of curiosity, both toward ourselves and toward the folks we are in relationship with. ❋ Ask questions like, "Why did my partner make this choice that I'm struggling with?" and "Why am I having this emotional response that doesn't align with my logic about what's going on?" or "What unconscious beliefs am I holding on to that no longer reflect how I wish to view love and relationships?" ❋ And sometimes the answers will scare us. They might show us our deep-seated desires to control or limit others due to our own lack of feeling safe and secure, or show us that the people we are in relationship with aren't who we thought they were. We may realize that our partners don't have what we want or need to continue being with them. But the fear of scary answers doesn't mean that we shouldn't ask the questions.

What have you discovered about yourself when you applied curiosity to your emotions?

Your partners aren't wrong for choosing partners they like and value with little to no consideration of whether or not you will like or value them, especially if having a "kitchen table" dynamic is of little importance to them.

It can be difficult when your partner chooses people you don't understand, or people you just don't vibe with, but they aren't wrong for choosing those people. Even if you're trying to adhere to a kitchen-table dynamic, sometimes, you just don't mesh well with a person even if your partner thought you would. You may not see what your partner sees in them and that's OK. You can manage your boundaries around interacting with their other partners and try not to judge them harshly for their choices. ❧ It is also OK to let a relationship go if your partner consistently chooses folks who are harmful to them or you, who create unnecessary issues or if a kitchen-table dynamic is important to you and you can't seem to enjoy any of your metamours. ❧ However, make sure to check in with yourself to see if it's really that your partner chooses people you don't vibe with or if you are subconsciously determined not to like anyone they interact with because you struggle with nonmonogamy.

Is it important to you that your partners choose people you like and get along with? Is it important to you to choose people you believe your current partners will like or get along with? Why or why not?

When you enter nonmonogamy with a partner you were previously monogamous with, it is likely you will discover things that you are not in alignment on about how to navigate nonmonogamy.

My husband and I were extremely incompatible for nonmonogamy with one another. The ways in which we felt it should be navigated rarely lined up. Now that we're separating and I'm dating again, one of the benefits is that I get to explore being nonmonogamous and connecting to folks who are in alignment with me about how it should function in our lives. I didn't have that opportunity with my husband because we entered nonmonogamy from monogamy and neither of us had any idea how the other would navigate it. ❧ If you entered nonmonogamy with a partner you were previously monogamous with, it is likely there will be ways you disagree on how you want your nonmonogamy to function. It's imperative to discuss what you disagree on and see if there is a middle ground where you both feel free to move how you want to while still being considerate of the other. Having differences of opinion doesn't mean you or your partner is wrong. ❧ This is also one of the advantages of entering into nonmonogamy from a place of being single—you get to figure out on your own how you want your nonmonogamy to function and can then seek folks with similar ideals.

If you entered polyamory from a monogamous relationship, did you discover that you and your partner had differing ideas about how you wanted to navigate it? If so, how did you address that?

On the one hand, we have the kinds of relationships we want. On the other hand, we have the kinds of relationships we believe we are worthy of. If you struggle to find what you want from relationships, examine what you believe you are worthy of having.

I had a conversation about this with a friend after a breakup. As they were examining the ending of the relationship, they realized that there were a lot of things they knew they didn't want in that relationship, but because there was some part of them that didn't believe they were able or worthy of what they wanted, they settled for less. ❧ How many of us know someone (or even are someone) who continuously complains about not having the relationships they want, but also constantly chooses relationships that are much less than what they say they desire? There is a difference between what we want and what we believe we are worthy of and usually, we pursue what we believe we are worthy of, even if we aren't fully conscious of that. ❧ Maybe you have an idea of the polyamorous relationships you want but you keep accepting less than that because you don't believe you can find more. If that's the case, it is likely coming from an internal belief that you aren't worthy of the relationships you truly want. If you believed you were worthy of them, you wouldn't give yourself anything less.

Is there a gap between what you want from relationships and what you believe you are worthy of? If so, what can you do to bridge that gap?

Not being up-front with someone who you are engaging with in a dating/romantic/sexual capacity about you being nonmonogamous removes their ability to consent to the interaction they are entering into with you.

Whether it's dating someone casually or dating someone with the intention of establishing a relationship, you should be up-front about being nonmonogamous, especially if you are already partnered. ❧ Many people respond with "Well, if I tell people I'm nonmonogamous, I won't have anyone to date," or "People stop wanting to date me when I'm up-front about it so I don't tell them right away." What they're saying is that they care more about getting what they want from a person than about giving them the opportunity to fully consent to the reality of the situation. It's a lie of omission. Yes, you may have a more limited dating pool if you're honest about your nonmonogamy, but at least you'll be engaging in connections that start from a place of honesty and transparency, some of the most basic tenets of nonmonogamy. ❧ Even for casual dating, some people would have a real problem knowing that they went out with a partnered person, even when the partner is OK with that. So, keep it real with folks. The right people will be all for the true you.

Have you ever had an experience where you weren't up-front with a person about being nonmonogamous and they reacted negatively when they found out? If so, what kept you from being up-front with them?

Sometimes, we only want something from our partners because we see that someone else is getting that from them, not because we actually want it. Make sure you are asking for what you genuinely want, not just trying to even the score.

Maybe you see your metamour post on social media that your partner sent them flowers. You find yourself feeling envious and thinking, "They never send me flowers." Then you remember that you don't even like flowers. Have you ever had an incident like this? ❀ It's human to compare. And it is possible to see our partners showing up to other partners in a way that we want them to show up to us. That's valid. It is also true that sometimes, it's not that our partners aren't doing the things we need them to do to help us feel special and loved, we just struggle with them doing those things for others. We can be kinda like the kid who was fine with the ice cream flavor he got until he sees that his brother got a different flavor. Now, the ice cream that was perfectly acceptable a few minutes ago isn't as appealing. ❀ If you are genuinely content with the relationship you have with your partner, don't make yourself discontent by unnecessarily comparing what you receive from them to what they give to others. Appreciate the individual way they love you.

How do your partners show up for you in personal ways that you appreciate?

Day 304

Before entering into relationships with partnered folks, ask about their thoughts and experiences with veto power and if they have a veto agreement in their relationships. It's an important discussion to have.

A veto agreement is an agreement made between partners that allows each the power to "veto" the other's relationship with another person. Once a veto has been issued by a partner, the other partner must end or drastically change their relationship with the person who was vetoed. This could mean breaking up with them, changing from romantic to platonic or ceasing a sexual relationship, among other things. ❀ I don't use much of my energy debating the ethical nature or validity of vetoes, but I will say that I never knowingly subject myself to relationships where I know a veto agreement is present. If you have a veto agreement, you should be telling folks that before you begin relationships with them. ❀ Unfortunately, some people have "sneaky veto agreements," meaning that they won't outright force a partner to break up with someone, but they'll make their life miserable about another relationship until their partner ends that relationship.

What are your thoughts and feelings on veto agreements?

Most relationship issues aren't matters of "right" and "wrong" but matters of perspective. A lot of relationship problems stem from a need to make someone wrong and someone right.

I remember when my husband told me that he made one of his partners an additional beneficiary on his life insurance policy. I struggled with his decision and while we didn't argue about it, there was some tense and difficult conversation around it. The thing is, he wasn't wrong for naming her as a beneficiary and I wasn't wrong for struggling with that. ❧ While there are issues in relationships that are matters or right and wrong, there are many issues that aren't—they are just differences of perspective. We often have to make the other person we're at odds with "wrong" or we make ourselves out to be "wrong" for how we see things when it's neither. It's just people being different. ❧ When we stop trying to make the other person wrong and ourselves right, or vice versa, we are more capable of holding space for their perspective and our own without needing to wrestle either perspective into submission. From that space, we can more readily find solutions that include both perspectives. Even in the example I mentioned above, where there was no middle ground or "solution" to be found, we came to a place of understanding each other because we weren't making the other one out to be wrong.

Is it important to you to designate someone as wrong and someone as right when you have conflict? If so, what keeps you from holding both perspectives as valid?

For some people, healing after a breakup looks like taking time away from forming new relationships for a while. For others, healing doesn't require that. Don't judge others' choices based on what is healing for you.

Often, folks advise people to abstain from relationships for a period of time after a breakup or judge people for moving on too quickly. People will say that the time they took in their own breakups was healing for them, so naturally this must work for everyone, right? ❧ When my marriage ended, my entire life was in a state of uncertainty and transition, and frankly, I felt like a conductor on the Hot Mess Express who had no business trying to date. But I considered my right to engage in connections and relationships that brought me joy while also working on putting my life back in order. Why couldn't I do this, especially if I was being honest with potential partners about my capacity? ❧ In polyamory specifically, we're often in multiple relationships at a time. One can end while you're still in another. After a breakup, you wouldn't expect a person to end all other relationships so they can focus on self and healing. Usually, they have to learn to do those things alongside being in their remaining relationships. ❧ A period of relationship cessation works for some and isn't necessary for others. What heals some, poisons another. Focus on what you need in the tender period after your relationships end and support others doing the same.

How do you encourage healing after a breakup?

If someone has clearly defined for you the limits of what they wish to have with you, and you accept less than what you want, it's not their responsibility to "let you go" because they can't or are unwilling to match your desires.

If someone clearly defines the limits of the relationship they want with you, and you accept what they offer knowing you want more, you can't then say they are leading you on or that they are responsible for ending things with you because they are unable to give you what you want. ❧ If this is something you're grappling with, ask yourself why you expect someone else to have more care and concern for your heart than you do? Ask yourself if you're accepting less in the hope that somehow you can be OK with it or are secretly hoping that you can be wonderful enough to make the person change their mind. ❧ It's probably the kindest thing you can do for yourself to tell them that you care about them but want more than what they're giving you and therefore need to move on. Don't wait for them to do it for you.

How do you handle mismatched relationship desires with a person you care about?

While you cannot choose who your partners decide to interact with, you can choose the level of interaction you have with the people they interact with.

It is not my place to choose who my partners are with, and I don't want my partners making those choices for me. While I may not see value in a particular person, that doesn't mean that my partner shouldn't see value in that same person. I also understand that my partners should be choosing people they enjoy and connect with, not people who appeal to me. It's not about me—I'm not the one they're dating. If I happen to have metamours I enjoy, I see it as a bonus benefit and not a requirement. ❀ When I have a partner who is interacting with someone I'm not fond of, I don't seek to control their relationship with that person but I can set boundaries in my interaction with that person. I figure out what my boundaries are and communicate them to my partner, be it limited interaction with that person to no interaction at all. I choose what I can do, not what they can do.

What are some boundaries you set when your partner has a partner who you don't wish to interact with?

People are allowed to want a different kind of relationship with someone else than the one they want with you.

Consider this example: Su and Jo have been in a relationship that's mostly casual for several months. They date when they have the time, have sex, converse every few days. Then Su meets Pat. Their relationship with Pat is deep and intense and soon after, Su and Pat start a committed partnership. Jo struggles with this. They feel hurt by the fact that their relationship with Su has remained casual, but that Su was ready to partner with Pat so easily. ❀ But Su didn't want that with Jo. Su wanted that with Pat. And ostensibly, Jo wanted the casual relationship they had with Su too, until Pat came along and Jo saw that Su was available for a more serious kind of partnership with someone, just not with them. Sound familiar? ❀ People are allowed to want different things with others than they do with us because different people inspire different desires. Yeah, sometimes that hurts to accept but it's still true. If we're struggling with the fact that someone is giving someone else a different type of relationship than they are giving us, it's likely that we aren't being honest about what our genuine desires are for our relationship and are accepting something different than what we truly want.

Have you ever experienced a similar situation? If so, how did that make you feel and how did you respond?

Often, when we are communicating with our partners about issues we're having with something they've done, in our minds, we've already tried and convicted them of trying to hurt us. Refrain from reaching a "guilty" verdict until you have collected all the evidence necessary.

When I'm upset about something that happens with a partner, I try to take the time to investigate before I make my judgment call. I usually find information that allows me to see that my partner wasn't trying to hurt me but was just making the best decision that they could see for themselves in that moment. ❧ If you communicate with someone from the vantage point of them already being guilty, it's no wonder that they become defensive about what you're saying. Try to communicate what you're feeling and the story you're being told by those feelings while also acknowledging that you know there is likely more to the story than just your perspective. Ask your partner what their viewpoint is so you can have a more informed picture of what actually occurred.

When you are upset with a partner, how can you remind yourself to suspend judgment before you have heard the entire story?

It can sometimes be difficult for non-nested or "secondary" partners to feel like an integrated part of their partners' lives. Making plans to do mundane things together can help to establish a feeling of life intimacy for these kinds of partnerships.

Years ago, I dated a couple and sometimes, when I was staying with them, we would go to the grocery store or run errands together. I would get almost as excited about those trips as if we were going on an actual date. I loved getting the opportunity to be present for the mundane and everyday things that were also a part of their lives. It made me feel closer to them. ❀ Being present for the mundane and day-to-day parts of our partners' lives is an important and underrated type of intimacy often not afforded to people who have partners they aren't nested/primary/married with. Time alone in the car on the way to an appointment, folding laundry together, working on a home or garden project with each other, tackling homework together, etc. are all little ordinary moments that can hold a lot of sweetness and closeness for folks in relationships. ❀ If you're struggling to feel like a substantial part of each other's lives, try carving out some time to do some of these things together. It can help to alleviate the feeling that your relationship with one another is purely about fun. It's also totally OK if this is not important to you and you don't want to do this in your relationships.

What mundane things do you enjoy doing with your partners?

When you're experiencing difficulty in your relationship with a partner, resist the urge to dissociate or "escape" from what's going on by getting wrapped up in newer, "easier" relationships or in existing relationships that are in a better place.

Rough patches are never fun and when a relationship is difficult or not meeting your needs, it can be tempting to avoid it by engaging in new relationships or by focusing on other relationships that are going better. ❀ However, this usually creates more problems because you're not present to deal with and work through what is happening. The partner you're having issues with is also likely to notice this dynamic and feel less cared for by you, resentful of your other relationships or like you don't value them and the relationship enough to navigate the difficulty with them. ❀ Other relationships can help us when we're experiencing difficulties—they can help us show up to relationship challenges from a calmer and satisfied place. But it's still important to show up to what is going on with all of our partners, not just the ones we are in a good place with.

How do you remain present in a relationship that is struggling when you have other relationships that aren't struggling?

When someone else opens your partner up to an awareness or experience that you wanted to open them up to, try responding with gratitude instead of resentment. The most important thing is that your partner opened up.

In my very first polyamorous relationship, our partner wanted my spouse to dress up for Halloween. I had been begging him to do so for years and he never would. Then she came along and all of a sudden he was more open to it. I was really resentful of that. This kind of situation is a common experience in nonmonogamy. ☀ My current partner has the best response to this—he says that while it causes him some crunchy feelings when a partner becomes open to something he wanted by their interaction with someone else, he shifts into gratitude that someone was able to reach his partner in a way he couldn't. Essentially, he moves his ego out of the way. ☀ We aren't the sole catalysts for change, growth and expansion in our partners. Others will be able to tap into them in ways that we can't. And if we're too caught up in the fact that it wasn't us who did it, we'll likely miss out on the benefit that it happened regardless.

Have you ever had a partner open you up to something that a previous partner tried to and couldn't? If so, what caused you to open up?

While we may believe that love is an infinite resource, time, energy, money and our bodies are not. And since these are all things we utilize to engage in relationships, we need to be mindful of their limitations.

"Love is infinite" is a platitude often heard in the polyamorous community. It's usually used to highlight that love isn't diminished by being shared, that love multiplies the more it is given away. It's saying that love is a resource that is unlimited. ❀ Whether or not you believe that is true, one thing that is definitely true is that the resources of time, energy, our bodies and our money are not unlimited. These resources have a limited capacity for sharing and that capacity is individual for each one of us. While I may have the room in my heart to romantically love twenty people, I definitely don't have the ability to show up for twenty romantic relationships well. Especially when you consider that I have other facets of my life that utilize those same resources and that I also have to reserve some of those resources for myself. ❀ So, love freely, but also love responsibly. Be mindful of what you are actually capable of giving in relationships and not burning yourself out in the process.

What does loving responsibly mean to you
in the context of polyamory?

It's OK to grapple with what to tell our partners about our interactions with others, even when we've had clear discussions about what to share with each other. Remember that you and your partners are doing your best.

Transparency looks different for different individuals and figuring out what to tell your partners is something we can all find challenging, even when we've talked about it and agreed on what we would share. What you define as significant information can differ from your partner's definition. ❧ Similarly, knowing exactly *when* to share some information can also pose a challenge. You might wonder if you're sharing something too soon after an event or not want to have a potentially uncomfortable conversation when your partner has had a rough day at work. ❧ Acknowledge that you and your partners are doing the best you can to be as up-front as possible while also holding room for the fact that misinterpretations, misunderstandings and missteps will occur.

When sharing with your partner about your interactions with others, what causes you anxiety?

It is not your responsibility to be the spokesperson for polyamory. It is simply your responsibility to live it in the best and most authentic way for you.

Being openly polyamorous while going through my divorce is hard. Even when they don't say it, I can feel that people are thinking, "Your marriage ended because of polyamory." I know that is far from the truth, but because I don't want to cast a negative shadow on polyamory, it hits me hard. ❧ But I also know it is not my job to represent polyamory in any other way than authentically to me. Other people's views of it aren't my responsibility to manage. I will not overly burden myself with other people's perceptions of my life. I could have everything going "right" in my polyamorous life and folks would still draw their own conclusions around it. I've released myself of the concern to shape other people's image of it. ❧ I am not obligated to be a representative of polyamory, and neither are you. Our duty to ourselves is simply to live it.

Do you feel obligated to be a representative of polyamory? If so, in what ways?

Don't spend so much energy worrying about whether someone likes you or if you work for them. Instead, consider whether you like them and whether they are compatible with you.

I'll start liking or dating a person and find myself thinking, "Maybe I'm not healthy enough for them" or "What if I'm too much for them?" This leads to anxiety, because really it boils down to "What if I'm not good enough for them?" It almost never crosses my mind to consider whether they are good enough for me. ❀ It's important to consider this and to not dwell on your own perceived shortcomings. Never forget that you are a prize, you are a catch and you are someone a person would be lucky to have.

Which do you consider more when forming a new connection with someone: whether you are a good fit for them or whether they are a good fit for you?

Day 318

Even as I identify that there are things about myself that I need to fix or work on, I also need to hold on to the truth that I am worthy of love and acceptance in my current state.

This is something I have to remind myself of during this time in my life. My marriage is ending, and I'm reformatting my entire existence and experiencing all the discomfort that comes with that. I feel like a mess. It's easy to tell myself that I'm not worthy of love, pleasure or people who choose me right now, at least not until I get myself together. ❧ Even in less turbulent times, it is easy to discount ourselves in a polyamorous context. We might tell ourselves, "I struggle with jealousy too much to be worthy of love," or "I don't know how to communicate well enough to be worthy of multiple relationships," or "I have too much trauma for multiple people to love me." It is important to acknowledge the ways in which we need to work on ourselves and improve but we do not need to perform penance for not being perfect by denying ourselves love. ❧ You are whole and complete even as you seek to improve and grow. And love has many forms that can fit you where you are now and grow with you as you grow. It's a both/and, not an either/or situation.

What things cause you to feel less worthy of love?

**Owning your choice to be polyamorous helps
you to feel empowered in navigating it, especially
during times of discomfort or struggle.**

This is something I remind myself of repeatedly, especially in times of difficulty. I am choosing to be nonmonogamous. I have made a conscious decision to be in relationships in this way and I accept what comes with my choice. I understand that dealing with discomfort or struggling through some aspects of my choice isn't the same as being victimized by my circumstances. I can also make different choices should I feel they better serve me. Nonmonogamy isn't happening to me; I am choosing it. ❀ Owning that you are choosing this makes accepting the challenges easier. You don't see them as things that are happening to you but as parts of the dance of nonmonogamy. That doesn't mean you accept anything that happens, but that you are aware of your agency. You can choose—you can choose relationships that feel nourishing to you, you can choose to create boundaries that help you feel safe, you can choose to stand up for yourself and your wants and needs and you can choose to walk away from things that don't work for you. ❀ I also want to acknowledge that for some people nonmonogamy isn't a choice but a part of their identity. This is valid. But even if that is the case, you can choose whether to practice it and how to engage with it. Even in cases of identity, there is still choice.

What does having agency in polyamory mean
to you? Do you find it hard to grasp your sense
of agency when things are difficult?

There's nothing wrong with being "information light" about your partners' relationships with others, but it's good to examine if that is coming from you needing or wanting to pretend your partner isn't with other people.

"Information light" is a term I use to refer to people who don't want a ton of info about their partners' relationships with others. Outside of logistical things, they'd rather not be made privy to the fine details of their partner's relationships with others. It's likely that they won't want to dish about their own dates, potentials and relationships either. There is nothing wrong with this, but I believe it is important to examine where this choice comes from. ❧ For some people it's simply about being private or indifferent, or the discomfort not being worth the knowing. For others, it can be a result of wanting to pretend their partner isn't with anyone else. That one is tricky. ❧ We do ourselves no favors when we don't acknowledge reality, especially if we've agreed to be polyamorous. Some folks accept it on a conscious level but continue to fight with it on a subconscious level. In this situation, any mention of their partners' other relationships can send them into a tailspin. Avoiding sharing details can be avoiding doing the deeper work of accepting their nonmonogamy.

Are you "information light" in polyamory? What is your level of comfort with your partners sharing about others?

Sometimes, it's not that our newer partners "get us" better or that our newer relationships are better than our older ones. It's that they don't have the years of history, hurts and ingrained relationship patterns that developed from partnering with folks when we were likely less mature and didn't know better.

One of my most difficult challenges in navigating poly-amory with my husband was envying his other partners because it felt like they had a more unobstructed pathway in their connection to him. We had been together for over a decade. We had kids, a life together, years of hurts and history, patterns that we had created in our marriage long before we were aware of them. All of that created what I call static or interference between us. His other partners didn't have any of that so their pathways to him were clearer. It was the same for me with my other partners. ❧ If you see your newer partners as "better," consider if what you're experiencing is a result of the relationship coming from a clean slate with them, of you being more mature in relationships now, of you getting a fresh start to set better patterns and make better choices in your relationships with people, or a combination of all of these elements. Perhaps thinking about this will change how you view your more established partnerships and help you to make some changes in them so they can be as exciting and flourishing as your newer partnerships.

What differences do you notice in your newer partnerships from your more established ones?

My primary concern in my relationships isn't how many other partners my partners have but that I am getting my needs met. As long as I can say that's true, the number of partners they have or don't have isn't my concern.

People often focus on the number of partners their partners have and make all kinds of judgments around that or even try to control it. You might hear, "You date too many people and I don't understand it. How many is enough for you?" or "You don't date enough. Why don't you get out there and find someone else?" ☙ The underlying concern of either of these is needs. If you're worried that your partner dates too much, it's likely that you are worried your partner will have too many people to tend to and you'll get lost in the shuffle. If you worry that your partner dates too little, it's likely that you are feeling guilty or are worried that their lack of partners means you won't get your needs for space and freedom met. ☙ Let your partners work out for themselves how many or how few other relationships work for them. Your primary concern for your relationship with them should be whether you're getting your needs met. As long as you can say that's the case, then their capacity for others is their business.

Do you have thoughts, feelings or judgments about the number of partners your partners have? If so, what are they?

If you're a nonmonogamous person and you choose not to engage in nonmonogamy because you have an unwilling monogamous partner, you can't say that they are holding you back. You are choosing the relationship you have with them.

I think it's very unfair for people to blame their partners for holding them back in nonmonogamy. You can absolutely live the nonmonogamous life you want—you just may not be able to do so with your current partner. Agreeing to be monogamous with someone and then claiming that they are holding you back from nonmonogamy makes them a scapegoat for you not living the life you want. It is a setup for resentment, and it likely wouldn't make your partner feel good to know that you feel that way about them. ❧ While it's OK to struggle with the choice you are making to be monogamous with someone, remember that it *is* a choice. You are choosing what is most valuable to you, which is to remain in the relationship with your monogamous partner. Own that. There is nothing wrong with that being more important to you than practicing nonmonogamy. ❧ Just don't make that decision and then complain about how your partner won't let you be nonmonogamous. It's not their job to grant you permission. It's your job to grant yourself that. And if that means you have to part ways because your relationship values don't align, that is sad but understandable. It wouldn't make either of you a bad person.

Have you ever felt held back from nonmonogamy by a partner? How did that affect your relationship with them?

It is important for every sexually active person capable of reproducing to take ownership of their own reproductive responsibility. Placing the fate of your reproductive responsibility in the hands of another person means you forfeit your reproductive autonomy.

If you place your reproductive responsibility in the hands of another person, you forfeit your power to have control over your reproductive decisions. All sexually active persons who have the potentiality to reproduce should take an active role in determining their own reproductive decisions to the best of their ability. I acknowledge that lack of access to healthcare, education and contraceptives can play a huge role in how effective a person can be in this. ❧ In nonmonogamy, it's particularly important to have detailed conversations about this topic. We should be asking our partners what their views are on having children overall, on having children outside of married/ nested dynamics, abortion, unwanted pregnancy, what contraceptive measures are being taken, vasectomies and other sterilization procedures for those who don't want kids and have access to those measures—the works. Often, polyamorous folks don't talk about this stuff until it's too late. ❧ And, if I can be frank, cis men should stop making it cis women's responsibility to think about this and manage it. Y'all need to be just as invested in this work as we are.

Have you had discussions with all your partners about reproductive responsibility? What safeguards have you put in place to prevent unplanned pregnancies?

You can do all the self-work in the world to manage your jealousy, unpack monogamous conditioning and develop healthy communication tools and it still may not change the fact that a person, or your relationship with them, isn't right for you.

You can think of your relationship as a stage on which you and another person are acting out a production. You can recite all of your lines perfectly and hit every cue with precision but if the other person on stage with you isn't also playing their part, it won't go well. ❦ There's an emphasis on self-work in nonmonogamy, and I agree with the importance of it. Learning to manage ourselves well in relationships is vital to our success in navigating them. But it's only one side of the equation. The reality is that for some relationships, there ain't enough self-work in the world to fix the fact that someone just isn't right for us, the relationship with them isn't right for us, or they are unwilling or unable to meet us with work of their own. ❦ In a former relationship I used to think, "If I could just figure out how to be less jealous and work on my emotions, I'll be good." I did all that and it still ended. The person wasn't right for me, and I wasn't right for them. When we are in relationships, we aren't the only one on the stage. It's a collaboration of the individuals involved, not a monologue or a soliloquy.

Have you ever ignored that a relationship or a person wasn't right for you by pursuing more self-work? If so, what was the end result?

Don't make your partners referees for your issues with your metamours. Be an adult and deal with them directly.

Speaking as a person who has done this very thing, it places your partner in a really uncomfortable and unfair position. Your partner shouldn't have to play mediator to you and their other partner, fielding messages between you or even facilitating mediations. One of the things I both loved and loathed about a former partner was that they refused to put up with my shit when it came to this. They would literally say, "I don't know, go ask them." It burned me up at the time but I knew it was the right thing to do.

Have you ever had two partners place you in the middle of an issue they had with each other? If so, how did that feel?

Day 327

It is your partner's job to communicate to others whatever relationship agreements they have made with you that have an impact on their other relationships. It is also solely your partner's job to uphold these agreements when they are engaging with others.

Consider this scenario: You and your partner make an agreement that you will not spend the night at the house of anyone else you are dating. Your partner begins dating someone new and they go out for an evening. Your partner didn't tell this new person about the agreement and the new person invites your partner over for the evening. Your partner goes, gets caught up in spending time with them, and doesn't come home until the morning. You are understandably upset. ❧ Often in situations like this, people will become upset with their metamours or the people their partners are seeing, but those folks usually have no idea that there was any agreement in place, and even if they do know, it's unfair to expect them to uphold an agreement they didn't make. ❧ It's not your metamours' job to check on what agreements your partners have with you or to hold your partners accountable to keeping those agreements. The responsibility of communicating those agreements and upholding them belongs solely to your partners.

Do you have relationship agreements with someone that impact your other relationships? If so, have you communicated those agreements?

Most people's "changing" in relationships is really them just being more honest with their partners and with themselves.

When we experience a partner "changing" in their relationship with us, is it that they really changed or that they became more honest with us about who they really are and who they really want to be in their relationship with us? This isn't to say that people don't change, but I believe that often what is actually happening is that they are deepening in their authenticity. ❀ Similarly, people often go into relationships holding up a mask of who they are and what they want us to see, designed with what they believe is lovable and valuable to us. After a while, though, their arms get tired. They can't hold the mask up forever. In this scenario it's not that they changed, but more that they changed themselves to be with us and are now returning to themselves. Let's engage in relationships where we can be the unmasked versions of ourselves, where we can rest and be at home in who we really are.

Are you being completely honest with the people you are in relationships with about who you are and what you wish to share with them? If not, how are you not being fully honest?

When weighing the choice to be honest and authentic with someone, shift the question from "Will I run this person off?" to "Why do I want to be in a relationship with someone I am afraid can't or won't embrace who I genuinely am?"

Lately, I have been examining my internal relationship narratives and changing some of the dialogue I have with myself. A common one I experience is the worry that I may be "too much" for someone and that if I'm genuine and honest with someone about my needs, wants, thoughts or feelings, I will scare them off. ❀ I have been paying attention to when I experience these thoughts and the emotions of that worry, especially as it relates to me simply being real with a person. I have realized that the real issue is not that I need to figure out how to adjust myself to keep them around but why I want to do myself a disservice by involving myself in relationships with people who can't or won't hold who I truly am. ❀ Relationships where I am unable to be authentic are built on falsehoods that will eventually come crashing down. And the fear of that will be such that I will never be able to feel secure in those relationships, or to experience ease and rest. I deserve to have folks who authentically embrace me, and so do you.

Do you worry about running people off by being the real you? If so, what do you think people can't handle?

An important part of personal accountability is owning when we act out. Not just by saying sorry when we behave poorly, but also by communicating our understanding of why our behavior wasn't acceptable, sharing what was influencing us and acknowledging the impact our behavior had.

People act out for a variety of reasons—feeling vulnerable and needing reassurance or not feeling like their needs are being met. Even being tired, stressed or hangry can cause people to lash out and behave in ways that they later recognize aren't OK. ❧ When we recognize that we acted out and behaved poorly, saying sorry is just one part of holding ourselves accountable. The other part is communicating our understanding of why what we did wasn't OK, sharing what was going on that prompted you to behave in the way you did and holding space for the impact your behavior had. ❧ It's the difference between saying, "I'm sorry I was rude to you when you came back from your date," and "I'm sorry I was rude to you when you came back from your date. I was struggling with you going out with that person because I had a rough day and was feeling stressed and could have used an evening cuddling and talking with you. I'm also feeling insecure about this new person because you have a lot in common with them and I worry that you will desire them more than me. What I said to you was uncalled for and I apologize for hurting your feelings."

How can a person demonstrate that they're holding themselves accountable?

Day 331

Be mindful of the environments you bring your partners into and don't subject them to situations where they may be abused or disrespected by partners, friends or family members because you want to "live out loud."

This is especially important if your partners belong to a marginalized identity. You shouldn't sacrifice the comfort and safety of your partners in the name of living your polyamorous truth. If you know you have family members, friends or even other partners who are unsafe for your partners to be around, don't subject them to harm in the name of wanting everyone to "come together." ❦ Also, don't bring your partners around and then spring "coming out" on your family and friends with them present. Coming out as nonmonogamous is a separate conversation to have with your loved ones. It is unkind to subject your partner to the discomfort and surprise that their presence will bring when you share the big news. ❦ If you plan on having your partners around your family and friends for the holidays or an event but concealing the nature of your relationship with them, you should have that conversation with your partners beforehand to make sure they are OK with essentially having to hide who they are to you.

Have you ever had a partner bring you into an unsafe environment? If so, what made it unsafe? How did you handle it?

When you think your partner is being "better" to someone else than they are to you, examine if that's what is actually happening or if there are other reasons causing you to perceive their treatment of another as better.

I remember once having a conversation with a metamour about a frustration they were having with our partner around scheduling. It was oddly comforting. While I absolutely want my partners to treat all their partners with the highest quality of care, that conversation showed me that in some ways, my partners are the same people with others as they are with me. My insecurities sometimes whisper to me, "They give the best of themselves to their other partners and not you." Learning that my partners are just as human in their other relationships helps me to feel more at peace and have more grace. ❧ When you find yourself thinking that someone else is getting a better version of your partners than you are, pause and reflect on if that's actually true. It could be, but it could also be that you are seeing things that way because you are feeling insecure. It could also be that how your partner operates works better for another person than for you (something I have also experienced). Don't just go with the first story your emotions tell you about this. Take a step back to examine.

Have your insecurities ever influenced you to see your partner's treatment of another person as better than how they treated you? If so, was your assessment accurate?

Not every instance of struggling with a partner's other relationships is about needing to be "better" at polyamory or do more work. It can also stem from not feeling fulfilled in your relationship with your partner.

I don't believe that compersion is necessary for polyamory. I also believe that our feelings are ours to work through and manage. However, speaking from my own experience, the relationships where I struggled with jealousy and envy most were the ones where it was a struggle to be supportive of my partners feeding others because I felt like I was starving in my relationship with them. ❧ I was once in a relationship in which I felt like I was in a constant state of low-grade hunger. I got just enough to keep going, but I rarely felt full. It made being supportive and happy about my partners' other relationships damn near impossible. It's hard to watch someone feeding others when you're feeling hungry in your relationship with them. ❧ If your needs aren't being met by someone, it's hard to know they are meeting the needs of others. Consider what is really going on and how you can address it. It could be that you aren't communicating your needs well or at all, it could be that your partner can't provide for your needs even with valiant effort or it could be that they don't want to give those things to you. Whatever the reason, not getting your needs met will influence how supportive you can be of your partner's other relationships. That's just human.

What things have you noticed make it harder for you to be supportive of your partners' connections with others?

Some people are easy to love but hard to be in a relationship with. The two don't always go hand in hand.

Have you ever heard the saying, "Be with someone who doesn't make you feel like you're hard to love"? I reflected on this and some of my former relationship experiences. What I found was that I rarely struggled to love the person. Loving them was easy. It was loving being with them that was hard. ❀ When my husband broke up with me, the one thing he said that made accepting his choice make sense to me was that he no longer believed in the notion that relationships should feel hard. We had always had a hard relationship. We loved each other easily but it was hard being together. ❀ I find this to be a difficult space. Do I choose loving the person or believing I deserve ease in my relationships? I am currently working on building relationships in which loving the person and loving my relationship with them comes easily.

What are your beliefs about relationships being hard? What hardships are you willing to endure and what hardships are you unwilling to endure in relationships?

Having multiple situations in your life that draw on your emotional reserves will affect how centered you can be when navigating polyamory. Keep this in mind for yourself and when dealing with your partners.

Along my journey I have noticed that depending on what's going on in other areas of my life, my ability to be as centered as I'd like to be in polyamory fluctuates. If I'm dealing with a work issue, a parenting struggle or financial problems, something like my partner starting a new relationship or going on a date might be more challenging for me because my emotional reserves are being drained in other areas. ❧ It's important to remember that even when life pulls on our energy in areas that don't deal with our relationships, our relationships will still feel the impact. You might normally be fine with your partner meeting someone new but if you just lost your job, broke up with someone or got sick, you may struggle to be as calm and supportive as you normally would be because you're going through a lot in other areas. ❧ It's also important to keep this in mind when dealing with our partners. This isn't to say that we need to alter our behavior or choices, but if your partner is going through a lot, they may struggle a bit more than usual with your relationship and with others. Be empathetic and acknowledge the space they are in.

How do you maintain your polyamorous integrity when life challenges make it harder?

It's difficult to hold space for your partner's emotions in polyamory if you're judging them for even having them in the first place.

People often ask me how to deal with a partner's jealousies, insecurities or uncomfortable emotions in order to be more supportive and empathetic. I find that judgment of the fact that their partners are having emotions to begin with or judgment for which emotions they are experiencing gets in the way of people holding space and accessing empathy for their partners. ❀ If you are judging your partner's emotions, you can't empathize with them. You can't hold space for something that you believe shouldn't be there to begin with. Your judgment will be expressed and felt, and it will be an obstacle to you connecting to your partner. It's OK to struggle to understand the presence of particular emotions, especially if they aren't ones you believe you would experience in the situation. You can even express that you don't understand, as long as it's without judgment. ❀ If you find yourself struggling to be supportive of your partner in their emotional state, examine if you are judging them for even being there to begin with.

Do you judge some emotions? If so, which ones and why?

Couple privilege is at an all-time high during holiday seasons. Make sure you are checking in and making room for all the people you are in relationships with to help them feel cared for and important, not just your "main" partner.

From deciding on plus-ones for holiday parties to going away with your spouse for weeks to see family, and from being unable to see partners on the important days of the holidays to only getting gifts for your primary partners, couple privilege runs rampant during the holidays and single and solo-polyamorous folks usually get the short end of the holiday peppermint stick. ❄ Make sure that you check couple privilege and collaborate with all your partners on ways to help them feel special to you during these times. Consider of all your partners' needs and desires during holidays and remain flexible and open to creating traditions and engaging in activities that make all of your partners feel honored by you.

What plans do you have in place to ensure that all your partners feel cared for and included during holiday seasons?

Everything that irritates us in polyamory has the potential to lead us to a deeper understanding of ourselves if we apply a spirit of inquiry to it.

Carl Jung said that "Everything that irritates us about others can lead us to an understanding about ourselves." I have found this to be particularly true for my polyamorous journey. I always say that the biggest benefit of polyamory for me is self-discovery. When I inquire into why I'm unsettled by something my partner is doing, I always discover something within me that I can bring consciousness to. ❀ Sometimes it's an old wound that still needs healing, or an insecurity that I wasn't aware of. Sometimes it's a new awareness of a value or need I have that my partner isn't meeting. Sometimes it's a necessity to go deeper in my awareness of self-worth and to stand up for myself when I'm not being treated well. Sometimes I have realized that I am seeking to control others in a way that is not in alignment with who I ultimately desire to be. ❀ Irritations have been the source of tremendous lessons for me about who I am, what I believe about myself, what I value and desire, what I need to feel cared for and safe in relationships with others and where I need healing and growth. Though they don't feel great in the moment, I have come to accept and even have gratitude for these instances and approach them curiosity when they arise.

Think about something that irritates you in polyamory. What is a deeper understanding of yourself that this irritation shows you?

It's OK to never want to live with a particular partner or any partner. It's OK to choose the partner you feel is best suited for you to nest with, and it's OK to have a desire to nest with someone but acknowledge that your current partner isn't compatible for that.

When my marriage first ended, I was sure that I wanted to have another nesting partner again. Now that I've lived on my own for a while, I like the freedom and peace that comes with not living with a partner. While I know I don't want to live alone forever, I'm now not so sure I want to live with a partner. ❦ Our culture pushes that we have to get to a point of living with our romantic partner, and that this makes the relationship "serious." But this is just not true. It is absolutely OK to never want to live with a romantic partner and still believe that you can have serious intimate partnerships. It is absolutely OK to want to have a nesting partner, to accept relationships with folks who don't want that with you and to seek others who do want that with you. It is also OK to have multiple partners and decide that a particular one is the one best suited for nesting with—it doesn't necessarily mean you see your other partners as "less than." Finally, it is also OK for your thoughts and feelings on cohabitation to change as you move through life.

What are your desires around living with partners or others? Have your desires changed over the course of your polyamorous journey?

If you have partners who struggle with opening up to you, resist becoming impatient with them. Impatience can be felt and is counterproductive to them feeling safer and opening up to you.

File this under things I wish I could go back and tell my former self. I used to be in a relationship with someone who struggled to open up and let me in. Because I deeply desire closeness and intimacy, I would get frustrated and impatient with them, especially around the necessary emotional conversations we would have. Openness is easy for me and I couldn't understand why it was like pulling teeth to get this person to share with me. ❀ When you have partners who struggle with vulnerability, you need to create an environment that feels safe. You can do this by being patient and caring for them. It's likely that they're struggling to open up because they already don't feel safe and any sense of judgment, frustration or impatience can exacerbate their feelings. You can be honest about your struggles with their closed-off nature but it's important to express that in a way that doesn't communicate that there is something wrong with them or imply that they owe you entrance into the deepest part of themselves. ❀ In nonmonogamy, it's also important to recognize that you may have one partner who is extremely open and shares easily and others that are less so. Adjust your awareness and approach to the person you are dealing with.

Do you become impatient when you have a partner who struggles to open up? If so, why? If you're a person who struggles to open up, how does it feel when people are impatient with you about it?

If our partners withdraw while navigating discomfort about our nonmonogamous choices, it can be hard not to take that personally or find it to be hurtful.

When I'm navigating a discomfort in polyamory, I can become withdrawn and cooler than my naturally warm and connective self. When this happens, my partners can feel slighted by the change in temperature they feel from me. Their reactions can include sadness, guilt, shame and defensiveness, and these reactions can make it even harder for me to process my feelings. What I wish they would understand is that I still love them and want to connect to them, but I need time to settle myself. ❋ If your partner withdraws as they are processing some discomfort, it's OK to have your genuine feelings about that but understand that they're just doing what they can to navigate their emotions. Try not to take it personally, be supportive and let them know that you will be there when they are ready to reconnect to you. And please, don't badger or press them to talk or connect before they are ready to. ❋ If you are the one feeling the need to withdraw, communicate that. Nothing is worse than your partner sensing something is up with you and asking about it and hearing, "I'm fine." Note that this isn't referring to instances where someone is being hostile or punitive in their withdrawal.

Do you experience hurt feelings when your partners withdraw from you? How do you communicate with them about this?

Find your authentic dating lane in polyamory. What works and feels good for your friends and your partners may not always be what works or feels good for you.

In this age of dating apps, meetup groups and speed dating, there are loads of ways polyamorous folks can find people to connect with. But if you're an introvert, not a big fan of online dating or just plain shy, you can often find yourself looking around at your partners' or your friends' dating successes wondering if you should be doing what they are doing to meet and connect with folks. ❧ It's important to find a way to navigate dating that feels most comfortable for you. While I believe there's merit to stepping out of our comfort zones and trying new ways to connect, trying to mirror the successes of others by doing the same things they do will only result in us feeling frustrated and wanting to give up if they aren't how we genuinely wish to interact. ❧ Do what works for you, what makes you feel good and what is most comfortable and authentic to how you genuinely desire to meet people. Find your unique way to navigate dating, try not to compare yourself to others and just focus on being you.

How do you differ from your partners
in your approach to dating?

Day 343

Learn the difference between someone attempting to control your nonmonogamy and someone asking you for a consideration. One seeks to limit your behavior. The other asks that you modify your behavior in a way that aids your partner in supporting you.

This is the difference between your partner saying, "Can you not post any other partners besides me on your social media page?" and them saying, "When you post your other partners to your social media page, would you mind changing the settings so that I can't see it because it makes me uncomfortable?" ❀ One asks you not to do something you may have wanted to do. The other allows you to do what you want while being considerate of your partner's sensitivities. ❀ Not every request that our partners make for consideration or accommodation is an attempt to control us. Often, they are requests that enable them to feel considered and supported as we do something. They aren't trying to limit us. Rather, they are trying to ask us to meet a need they have as we go. ❀ It's important to remember that we can negotiate, make a different suggestion or say no when a partner asks us for a consideration we do not wish to provide.

How does it feel when your partners ask you for considerations? Do you perceive it as them trying to control or limit you?

Much of the language we use to communicate to others and to ourselves about our relationships suggests ownership of our loved ones. Reframing the language we use to talk about our partners helps us to shift this perspective.

I am often asked what it's like to "share" my partners. I always reply that I don't share them because sharing them implies that they are a possession of mine and they don't belong to me. My partners are human beings who are free to decide who to give themselves to and how. ❧ Much of the language we use to talk about relationships suggests ownership of the people we love. When we speak in terms of ownership of our partners, we then feel entitled to the relationship we have with them and what we want from it. That sense of entitlement can make it more difficult for us to be supportive of them giving to others what we believe "belongs" to us. ❧ Developing a new language that removes the implication of ownership helps to reframe our thoughts about our partners and who they are to us. And changing your thoughts paves the way for your feelings to change too.

Have you considered the language you use to talk about your relationships? If so, have you made any changes?

If you struggle with the need to be first in your partner's life, shift your mindset from needing to be most important to being important, from most special to being special, or from first to being a priority.

In monogamy, you choose one person above all others to be in a relationship with, essentially making them the most important, most special person who comes first in your life. It's no wonder that when people come to polyamory, they struggle with feeling insecure unless they are "first" in their partners' lives, coming before the other important people their partners are in relationships with. ❀ Unless you have a hierarchical relationship dynamic with your partner, holding on to the need to be first will be a source of suffering as you try to accept your partners' autonomy and right to choose to prioritize their individual relationships as they genuinely see fit to do so. Sometimes, you'll be first, sometimes someone else will be. ❀ Instead of getting upset that you aren't first, try instead to be at peace with being a priority, not needing to be the most important person to your partner but being content with being *an* important person to your partner. Letting go of your need to be the most special person to your partner creates room for their other relationships to feel important, too. And understanding that your partners can prioritize others and still highly value you helps you to feel more secure in polyamory.

Is it important to you to be "first" to your partners? Why or why not?

Day 346

The number of partners we have isn't an indicator of how skilled we are at polyamory.

Measuring how adept you are at polyamory by the number of partners you have isn't necessarily an accurate gauge of how successful you are at it. It also means that you'll likely seek to collect multiple relationships just to prove to yourself that you can have them, not because you have the drive, desire or capability to maintain them. ❦ The number of partners you have has no bearing on how polyamorous you are or how good at it you are. To use the old cliché, it's better to focus on quality over quantity. Even if you only have one partner, you are still polyamorous. It's best to have the number of partners you know you can show up well for. You are no less polyamorous if you are single, have only one partner or limit yourself to a small number of romantic relationships because you don't have the bandwidth for more. ❦ Skill in polyamory is about much more than just how many relationships we can be in simultaneously.

Do you feel as self-assured in your nonmonogamy when you are single or only have one partner? Why or why not?

Sometimes we hold on to a relationship for far too long and by the time we let it go, so much damage has been done that there is nothing of what was good about it left to salvage. Learn to let go.

It is almost always difficult to decide to let go of a relationship. Perhaps we don't want to give up or we care about our partner and don't want to lose them even if it's not working out. We can be afraid that we may not come across love again if we end things or want to believe that we can figure out how to make things work. ✤ I often find that people will hold on to relationships that aren't working for too long and by the time someone finally lets go, so much damage and pain has taken place that nothing is left to be salvaged. If you hold on too long, it may result in the unnecessary loss of a person you care for. If you'd ended things sooner, you might have been able to maintain some kind of loving relationship. ✤ Ask yourself, "If I make the choice to let go of this person now, will I still be able to say that I can appreciate who they are and the time we spent? If I don't let go and I stay, do I believe I will come to a point where I am so hurt by this person that I can't appreciate who they are anymore?" The answers to those questions can help guide you in what you need to do.

What are your personal indicators of when it is time to let go of a relationship?

Embrace the understanding that you are whole and complete exactly as you are and still, for some, you won't be enough.

One of my personal polyamory sayings is "I am enough for me." I may not be everything that my partners want and need in a person, but I am everything I need to be for me. ❋ The only person I can truly be enough for is me. I am complete exactly as I am. It's great when that works for someone I care about but sometimes, it does not. When I am not enough for someone I desire, it can be hard not to internalize that as "I am not enough," period. ❋ I have to remember that it isn't either/or but both/and. It is both true that I am enough for me and sometimes, I simply don't work for someone. Understanding this doesn't take whatever pain I may feel about this away, but it does help me to not reject myself because someone else did.

How are you "enough" for you?

**I am learning to look for red flags in myself.
If I find myself overall feeling poorly about
myself in a relationship, that's a red flag.**

I find it much more effective when, instead of looking for red flags in others, I look for red flags in myself. One glaring red flag I pay attention to is when I find myself feeling bad about myself in a relationship. If I'm in a relationship and I find it too hard to feel good about myself with that person, it usually means I don't feel secure with them. Whether it has something to do with their behavior or mine, it's highly likely that the relationship needs to shift significantly or end altogether. Relationships like that do a number on my self-esteem and that's a price I'm unwilling to pay. ❦ These are some questions I ask myself when I'm grappling with this:

◆ Am I proud of myself in this relationship?
◆ Does this person confirm what I affirm
about myself and in what ways?
◆ Do I feel like my relationship with this person
demonstrates that I have respect for myself?
◆ Does this relationship help me
feel good about who I am?

What red flags can you identify in yourself?

Polyamory can not only revolutionize the way we engage in romantic relationships, but also revolutionize the way we engage in all relationships. Don't be surprised if you feel a shifting in your other relationship spaces.

I was once in a triad, and we all lived together with my children. One morning, I got my feelings hurt by my daughter requesting for my partner to do her hair and not me. I called my husband on my way to work crying about it and I was literally sobbing into the phone "They're *my* kids!" ❀ I heard a little voice in my head that whispered, "No, they're not." My children don't belong to me. They are little humans who were placed in my care, but they aren't "mine." I credit polyamory for giving me this awareness, which enables me to be a better parent. ❀ Polyamory doesn't just affect how I operate in my romantic relationships, but how I operate in all my relationships. In learning to love my partners more freely, I have learned to love more freely overall. In learning to respect their autonomy, I have learned to validate the autonomy of everyone I care about. In learning to develop a stronger boundary ethic in my romantic relationships, I have strengthened my boundaries across all of my relationships. All my relationships have been improved because of it.

How has polyamory affected the relationships in your life that aren't romantic? Has it changed how you operate in them?

Day 351

One person's "clinginess" is another person's "holding on." One person's "too distant" is another person's "creating space in the relationship to breathe." These terms are subjective and instead of trying to define what they are for others, define what they are for you.

Clingy. Needy. Distant. Unavailable. These are all terms we hear often in relationship conversations, but if you asked ten different people how they would define what these things mean to them, you'd likely get ten different responses. ❀ Someone who is "clingy" to us may see their behavior as holding on firmly to keep the relationship intact. To the right person, their clinginess might be greatly appreciated and desired. Someone who is "distant" to us may see their behavior as allowing room to breathe in the relationship and to the right person, their distance could be a breath of fresh air. ❀ Defining what terms mean for us helps us to more easily discern when someone doesn't work for us without making it about that person being a faulty person. We can understand and accept that they are who they are but not what we need. It also helps us to find the folks who do work for us, the folks who are "just right."

Have you ever been called clingy or distant? If so, did you agree with the person about their assessment of you? How did it make you feel to be seen as such?

Day 352

We don't "share" our partners, because they don't belong to us. Our partners share themselves with us. And they can choose to share themselves with others in whatever way they deem best.

When my husband first introduced the concept of poly-amory to me, I was resistant to it. I didn't want to share him with anyone. I saw his affection, attention and regard as mine and I didn't want anyone else to have them. When we made the transition to polyamory, this mindset made navigating accepting his relationships with others very challenging for me. ❀ I have now come to understand that I don't share my partners' affection, attention and regard with the other special people in their lives because they don't belong to me to begin with. Those things belong to them and they share them with me and anyone else they choose to. I learned to be grateful that I was a recipient of that. ❀ This new mindset also helped me to feel less entitlement to my partners and more gratitude for them, seeing what they freely gave to me as a gift and not a right.

Do you consider yourself to be sharing your partners with others? How does that mindset affect how you think and feel about their relationships with others?

Sometimes, it's not that people are incompatible with each other but that the relationship structure they are in isn't compatible. Being open to changing the structure creates opportunity for them to find a relationship that more readily works for them.

Someone once told me it's not so much that there are incompatible people but that there are incompatible relationship structures for them. It made me reflect on my marriage. My husband and I definitely weren't compatible to be spouses anymore, but perhaps we could have been friends if we had been open to changing the structure of our relationship with each other. ❀ One of the things I appreciate about polyamory is that it opens up the opportunity for us to re-envision traditional relationship structures and create broader structures of relationships that allow us to retain people we care about in our lives. We don't have to suffer the needless loss of someone who matters to us simply because the relationship we were attempting with them didn't function well. We can explore different structures until we find one that fits.

Have you ever changed the structure of a relationship that wasn't working and then experienced more compatibility with the person as a result? If so, what about the change helped?

You can be over someone, but not over the relationship you had with them. Conversely, you can be over the relationship you had with someone, but not over them.

I started dating someone not too long after my husband and I broke up. I felt like I was ready for new love and that because I was out of love with my former spouse, I was mostly over my relationship with him. He and I were together for almost seventeen years. Naive, much? ❧ When that relationship ended, I realized all the ways that my hurt from my marriage influenced my behavior in the newer relationship, and I was shocked. I erroneously believed that being out of love with a person is synonymous to being over the relationship with them. I now know that those are two completely separate things. ❧ On the flip side, you can be in love with a person and yet be over being in a relationship with them. These things don't go hand in hand. ❧ Both of these states require awareness and healing. Make sure to examine what's really going on and take the time and space you need to reflect.

Have you ever been over a person but not over your relationship with them? Have you ever been over a relationship but not over the person you were in it with? If so, how did you realize this was what was going on?

Day 355

Relationship agreements are most successful when they are clear, flexible, not made under duress or coercion, able to be renegotiated and only expected to exist as long as they serve the needs of the people in them.

Relationship agreements are a common practice in polyamory, and they can be helpful to navigating nonmonogamy in a way that feels safe. They can also be the source of confusion, conflict and pain when they aren't properly managed. ❋ Agreements are most successful when they include clear definitions and when there are clarifying conversations to ensure a shared understanding. Flexibility for special circumstances and not holding the terms of the agreement too rigidly can also be useful. ❋ Ensure that all parties come to the agreement from a centered place and not from a place of coercion. All parties should also be able to discuss the terms and negotiate adjustments as they suit their needs and desires. Agreements should only last as long as the people included feel served by them. When that is no longer the case, there's freedom to get rid of the agreement altogether or create a new one.

What are your feelings on relationship agreements? Do you have any with your partners? If so, do they meet these guidelines?

Running from our uncomfortable emotions means we won't receive the messages they are trying to give us, which limits our opportunities to grow.

So many people want to avoid the uncomfortable emotions of polyamory. They look for anything they can do to avoid feeling uncomfortable. And I understand why, because the uncomfortable emotions I've faced in nonmonogamy have been some of the most visceral emotional experiences I've ever had. ❀ One thing I have learned about my uncomfortable emotions, though, is that they usually have a message to give me. They alert me to issues I need to address, sometimes with my partners, sometimes within myself, sometimes within my life or within the relationship. They also make me aware of places where I need to grow. ❀ If I run from my feelings or try to avoid them at all costs, I won't be able to hear what they are trying to tell me, and I'll miss the opportunity they are affording me to expand. I don't chase uncomfortable emotions, but I also don't run from them when they arise. I know they have a purpose and I have learned to appreciate that.

What challenges do you experience when facing your emotions? What are some subtle or not-so-subtle ways that you use to avoid facing them?

Feeling loved by someone isn't the same as feeling desired by them. Ask your partners what specifically makes them feel desired and communicate to them what makes you feel desired.

I've had a few relationships in which I knew my partner loved me and I could easily feel their love, but I struggled to feel desired by them. Some of that was my own insecurities and lack of belief in my desirability. Some of that was because my partners didn't show their desire for me in ways that I could readily perceive. We didn't speak the same language when it came to communicating desire. ❧ Since what makes us feel desired won't be the same as what makes our partners feel desired, it's important to have conversations about this. Ask questions like, "How important is it to you to feel desired in our relationship?" "What specifically can I do to show you I desire you?" "What things make you feel undesired in a relationship?" or "How do you communicate your desire for me?" ❧ Also, share what specific actions help you feel desired (if that's important to you). Telling them how you communicate your desire for them and talking about what desire means to you can help equip your partners with the tools to give you the feeling of desire that you need. Assuming that you and your partners experience desire in the same way sets you up for disappointment and misunderstanding each other's cues.

What actions make you feel desired by your partners?
How do you communicate your desire for them?

There is no one specific trait that makes someone "good" at polyamory. Each of us has attributes that help us navigate polyamory more easily and attributes that make navigating polyamory more challenging.

Lack of jealousy is usually seen as the most certain indicator that someone is "good" at polyamory. While a lack of jealousy can make navigating polyamory easier, lack of jealousy isn't an indicator that someone will be "good" at polyamory and experiencing jealousy isn't an indicator that someone will be "bad" at it. Jealousy is just one facet of dealing with nonmonogamy. Good time management, strong boundary setting, thoughtfulness and communication skills are just some of the other necessary tools that also contribute to polyamory success. We all have a combination of things that are strengths for us in polyamory and things that we need to work on. ❀ Additionally, try to move away from seeing a person experiencing jealousy as them being "bad" at polyamory. Jealousy is a normal human emotion. It's how we respond to it that counts.

What do you excel at in polyamory? What is more challenging for you?

If your partners have issues they want to address with you, don't dismiss them as being jealous. Not every issue they experience is about them feeling jealous and even if they are feeling jealous, that doesn't invalidate the issue they're having.

Dismissing your partner's issues as them "just being jealous" can be a form of gaslighting, and not giving credence to their concerns is uncaring. They can be completely at ease with your interactions with others and still need to address an issue that results from your other relationships. Plus, jealousy can alert us to things that need to be addressed, so if your partner is feeling jealous, it doesn't mean their issue isn't valid.

Has a partner ever invalidated your concern as just you being jealous? If so, how did you respond?

If we tell our partners we're going to work on something, we should also tell them what our specific plan is. Similarly, if we ask our partners to work on something, we should also suggest what specific actions we would like them to take.

Say you tell your partner you are going to work on communicating more. What does that mean? Are you going to be more open with them? Message them more? Be more detailed with what you tell them? Are you going to read some books on communication or work with a therapist? Just saying you're going to work on something is a vague declaration. Following up with how you're going to do the work demonstrates that you aren't just placating your partner but that you have a real plan for making a change. ❧ Similarly, asking your partners to work on something without suggesting what specific actions you'd like them to take is also vague and can be frustrating for your partners. They might not know how to give you what you want in the specific way you may be looking for. ❧ Being vague about improving your relationship doesn't instill a lot of confidence that you're on the pathway forward. It acknowledges a problem but doesn't offer solutions. Being specific about what needs to be done helps in feeling like progress is possible.

What was the last thing you said you'd work on in a relationship? What plan did you create to do so?

Understanding all the reasons why you are feeling something doesn't negate the actual need to feel it. Applying logic or intellectualizing our feelings won't always take the feeling away and doesn't take the place of feeling it.

I process my feelings very rapidly and I can usually get to the root of my emotions very quickly. While I'm grateful for that skill, I often find that I can get frustrated when I figure out where my feelings are coming from and yet the feelings persist. ❀ I will sometimes talk to someone about feeling jealous or insecure or threatened by something going on in their nonmonogamy and once we identify the cause of those feelings, they have the expectation that that alone should be enough to take the feelings away. They then become bewildered or sad and disappointed when it doesn't. This is because understanding an emotion is one thing and feeling it is another. ❀ You can't think your way through your feelings. Understanding how you feel is helpful to giving yourself grace and compassion, but you still have to *feel* your feelings. Instead of processing around your feelings, process *through* them. Allow yourself the time and space to feel what you're feeling.

How do you create room for yourself to feel your feelings? Do you spend more time thinking about your feelings than feeling them?

Not all partner choices are created equal. While we may be free to choose who we wish to engage with, those individual choices will not all land the same for our partners. Be mindful when choosing your partners.

It is one thing to meet someone at a bar, hit it off with them and then inform your partner that you have decided they are someone you want to pursue. It's another thing entirely to tell your partner that you are experiencing a connection with their sibling, their ex, their best friend, their partner or someone who has wronged them and have chosen to pursue that. You're not wrong for making the choice, but that choice is going to have a much different impact on your partner than the choice to date a random person who they have no history with or feelings about. ❧ People often exercise their freedom to choose who they wish to pursue without acknowledging that their choices can have an impact on their existing partners. It's crucial to navigate these situations with understanding, care, compassion, empathy and awareness. Treating your partner as if you don't understand why they may be struggling or as if they have no right to be struggling isn't really showing up to the situation with care for them. Validate their struggle and move in consideration and mindfulness.

How do you feel about your partners choosing to date your friends, exes or family members? Have you discussed your boundaries about partner choices with them?

For some people, labeling a relationship is important and creates a sense of security. For others, labeling isn't important or desirable. Labels carry weight and are more than just words— they have individual meaning for each of us.

I was once in a romantic relationship and decided that we should transition to friendship. To me, what we enjoyed with one another felt more appropriate for a friendship and making this shift would enable me to accept what my partner was consistently giving me with more ease. As we continued as friends, it was startling to me how little changed in our interactions. Just the simple relabeling of the relationship brought so much relief and peace. ❦ The labels we use to communicate about our relationships are more than just words. They hold our assumptions, our expectations, our desires and our needs. They carry the weight of our beliefs, ideas and histories. It's important to understand what terms mean for us and to communicate that to our loved ones. Assuming that they mean the same thing for others as for us can result in misunderstanding and disappointment. ❦ If labels aren't important or desirable to you, communicate that, too.

Are labels important to you? Do they make you feel secure, or do they make you feel boxed in?

If you can, try shifting your relationship with your attachment wounds from one of ruler and servant to one of teacher and student. You don't have to let your wounds take control of you, but you can let them teach and inform you.

So often, I hear folks talk about becoming triggered in relationships and making statements like "I get triggered and then it just takes over." I have totally been there. There's nothing worse than being in the throes of jealousy or feeling threatened or abandoned and not being able to get through to yourself. If you have a history of trauma or abuse in relationships, or if you are neurodivergent or even just in a space of healing after a painful relationship, it is particularly easy for your triggers to take over and make it so that your centered self is no longer in the driver's seat. ❧ When you're experiencing this, try to take a moment to pause. See if you can say to yourself, "This thing hasn't surfaced to control me but to teach me something." Taking a moment to remember that the trigger belongs to you and not you to it, and that it's actually trying to alert you to something, can help you reclaim your power. ❧ Reframing your relationship to the things that set you off from one of helplessness to one of personal agency and empowerment builds your self-efficacy. Your relationships will benefit from your increased sense of empowerment too. ❧ Also give yourself grace. Working through what triggers us doesn't happen overnight; it's a constant learning experience and a continuous practice.

How do you restore your sense of power when feeling overwhelmed by something that triggered you?

Day 365

The relationships that you truly want are on the opposite side of fear.

We move through our relationships with so much fear—fear of being abandoned, of being rejected, of telling our partners what we genuinely desire in case they won't be able to provide it or it won't be embraced. In doing so, we dishonor ourselves. Fear is a protection mechanism, but it can also limit us from having the courage to go after what we truly want. When we neglect to name our genuine needs, we compress ourselves and settle for watered-down versions of what we truly want. ❀ I am not immune to this myself. I'm afraid of a lot of things when it comes to love and relationships—my insecurities being confirmed, experiencing a past hurt again, making the same mistakes, not finding what I want—there are so many things that strike fear into my heart. But I don't want to live and love from fear anymore. I will never know the joy of my genuine desires if I'm too afraid to reach for them in the first place. ❀ To me, love isn't something I want to experience timidly. I want to be bold in love, believe in its possibilities and be courageous when I approach it. Polyamory takes bravery. Let fear of love fall away.

What scares you about relationships? How can you release those fears and instead be courageous?

Index

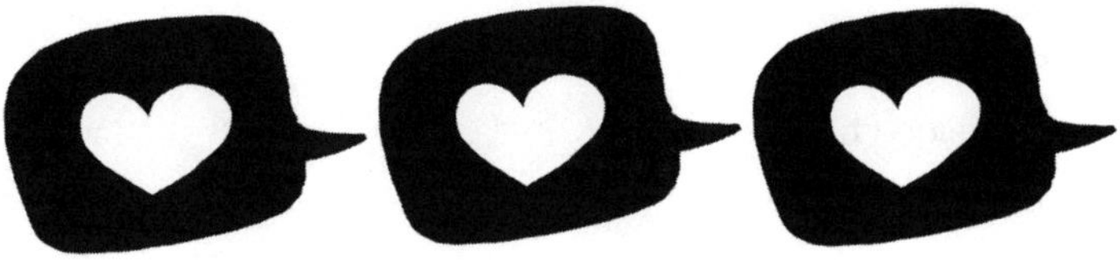

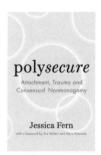

Polysecure:
Attachment, Trauma and Consensual Nonmonogamy
Jessica Fern

"*Polysecure* is smart, readable, pathsetting, and deeply caring. And practical. Jessica Fern presents abundant material that will inform poly-friendly therapists everywhere, and she offers six particular strategies that will help polyfolks and their beloveds to become more 'polysecure' in their relationships."

— Lindsay Hayes, Polyamory in the News

Love's Not Color Blind:
Race and Representation in Polyamorous and Other Alternative Communities
Kevin A. Patterson, with a foreword by Ruby Bougie Johnson

"Kevin does amazing work both centering the voices of people of color and educating white folks on privilege. His words will positively influence polyamorous communities for years to come."

— Rebecca Hiles, The Frisky Fairy

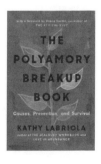

The Polyamory Breakup Book:
Causes, Prevention, and Survival
Kathy Labriola, with a foreword by Dossie Easton

"Mandatory reading for those considering an adventure into the world of consensual nonmonogamy."

— Ken Haslam, MD, founder of the Ken Haslam Polyamory Archives, the Kinsey Institute, Indiana University

Ask Me About Polyamory:
The Best of Kimchi Cuddles
Tikva Wolf, with a foreword by Sophie Labelle
"The warm and open style, and great way of getting
complex things across simply, makes it one of the best
relationship comics out there."
> — Dr. Meg-John Barker, author of *Rewriting the Rules*

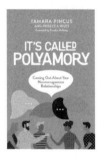

It's Called Polyamory: Coming Out About Your
Nonmonogamous Relationships
Tamara Pincus and Rebecca Hiles, with a foreword
by Kendra Holliday
"Doing poly, holding poly space in the world, is hard work,
often thankless. Thanks to this wonderful resource, it's
now a lot easier."
> —Loraine Hutchins, co-editor, *Bi Any Other Name:*
> *Bisexual People Speak Out*

Playing Fair: A Guide to Non-Monogamy for Men
Into Women
Pepper Mint
"Playing Fair is a brilliant road map for a more
conscientious approach to ethical nonmonogamy."
> — Kevin Patterson, founder of the *Poly Role Models* blog